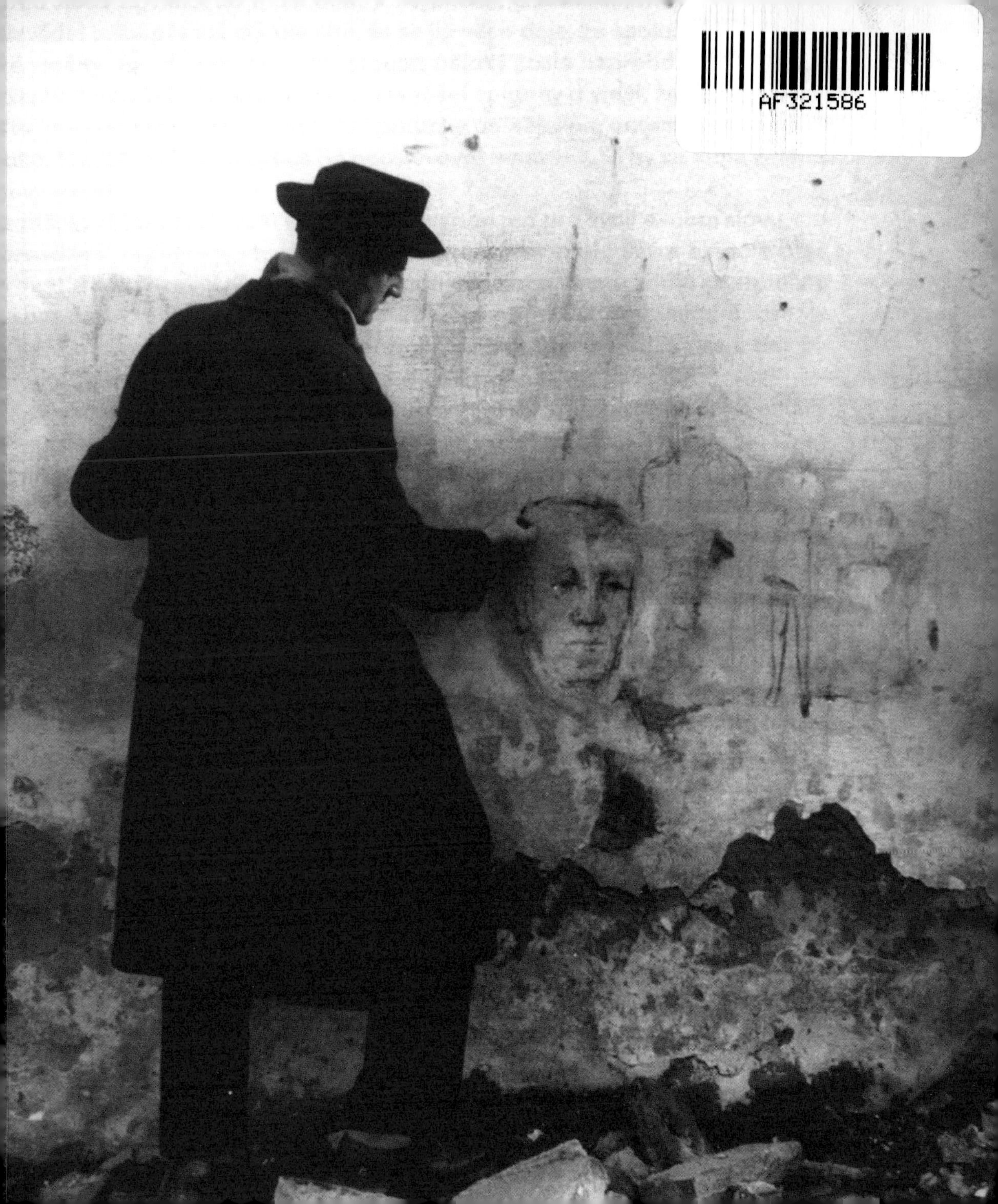

THE TENDER BARBARIAN

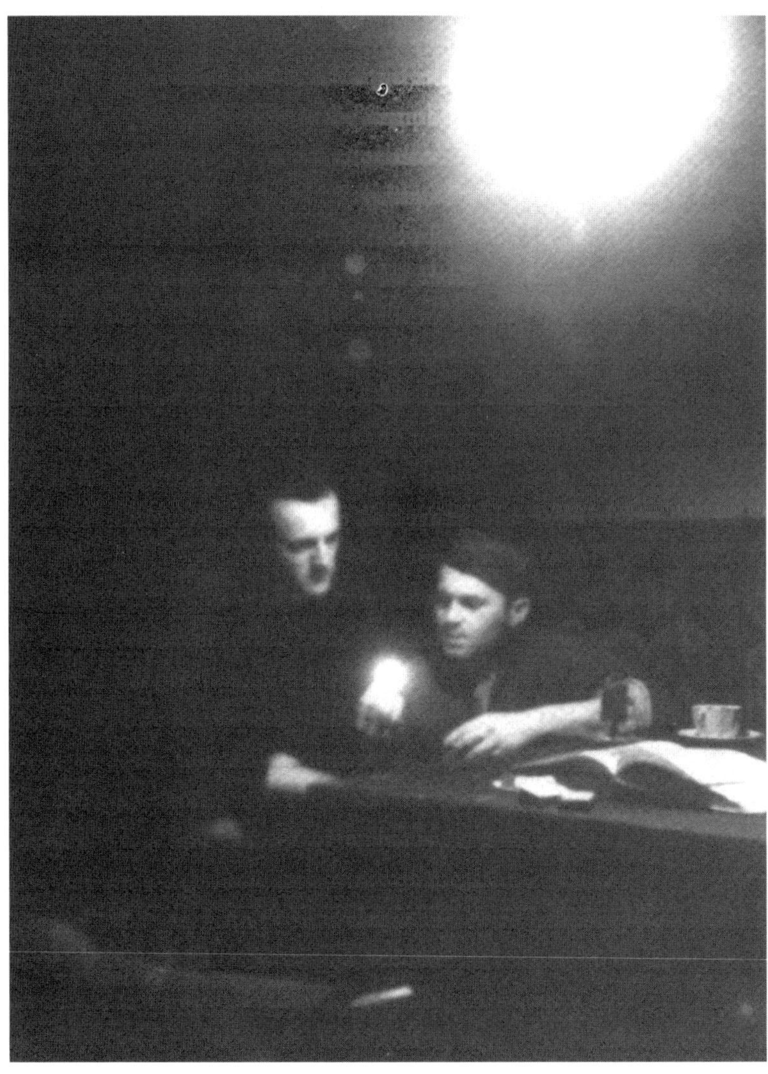

Vladimír Boudník & Bohumil Hrabal, Libeň, summer 1953

Bohumil Hrabal

THE TENDER BARBARIAN

Pedagogic Texts

*Artwork and Explosionalist Texts
by Uladimír Boudník*

Translated from the Czech by Jed Slast

TWISTED SPOON PRESS

PRAGUE

2019

The translation and publication of this book was made possible
by a grant from the Ministry of Culture of the Czech Republic.

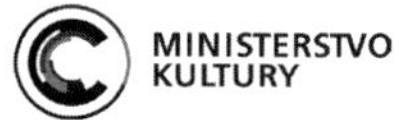

CONTENTS

How to Philosophize with a Hammer

— Friedrich Nietzsche

PROLOGUE

Vladimír loved the outskirts, he loved the permanently dug-up streets, their viscera of ripped out pipes, electric and telephone cables, all that black, swirling rebar with tentacles clutching terrified staid pedestrians like the serpents in the statue of Laocoön. Vladimír loved the piles of freshly baked bricks and flagstones randomly strewn on mounds of raw dirt — this method of revealing the bowels of a metropolis, and he likened the dug-up streets to his prints, always finding creative techniques in that clutter, so while he thought all those sewer pipes and electric cables, all those conduits and connectors should certainly be repaired, the whole of it should be left exposed, spanned by all those planks and hastily nailed together footbridges, like the kind found under St. Vitus Cathedral when another rotunda or chapel is discovered. Vladimír never tired of seeing that revealed beauty in which chaos has its order. I'm adopting his method to write this memoir of him, leaving the text like a dug-up street, and it's for readers to lay a plank or hastily constructed footbridge anywhere they please across the trenches of chaotically streaming words and sentences to allow passage to the other side . . . *Dichtung und Wahrheit*.

DIARY WRITTEN AT NIGHT

When Vladimír returned late at night from work, from his marvelous visits and encounters, he would lie down still fully dressed on his bed in the Prague district of Libeň, at 24 The Levee of Eternity Street. Bathed from above in the electric glow of a droplight fastened over his pillow, he wrote letters to himself, his diary. At that time Vladimír wrote his diary late into the night in a giant book resembling one of those ledgers in which breweries record the sale and production of beer, slaughterhouse brokers the sale and purchase of meat stock. Vladimír regularly recorded his daily events not because he wanted to, but because he had to, because writing was integral to his psychotherapy, because his hand in the act of writing ventilated the overheated furnace of his brain. He wrote his diary at night with a carpenter's pencil as his thoughts streamed so swiftly it required immense effort on his part to keep up with the flow of images haunting and consuming him. Usually he was attached to that book like a telephone book chained to a booth. So he scratched out his journal with the carpenter's pencil, devastated by a migraine hammering a nail into his head, by a gallbladder like a red-hot key unlocking his liver. Yet the more Vladimír wrote the more quickly his ailments and complexes faded. And when he would whoop his victory laugh several times a night, "Hahahahahaha!," the last wrinkles curled up behind his ears, his manic energy emitted its last sparks, and the workday came to a close only to continue on other planes and in other networks of delirious and hyperbolic dreams. At this time a quarter century ago when Vladimír was writing his diary at night, he often found himself in a morally paradoxical state, gurgling from brilliant associations to the true movement of matter through a narrow duct. Vladimír's intuition, his vision of new creative techniques, intensified his aggressiveness, which he grappled with from a prolonged adolescence to an adulthood that never actually came. As he was unable at this time to tease out the intrinsic aesthetic qualities of matter in a single step, that is, to break through from subjective individuality to universality and objectivity, he suffered from hypochondria and hysteria to such an extent that he escalated situations to the very brink of physical altercation, to the point of being sued for defamation. His letters to friends at this time were intended to offend, resulting not in eventual reconciliation and a return to their relationship as it had been, but in a synthesis, a higher identity, which Vladimír as creator again severed, so that this new rupture would attain even greater artistic and human cognition. Via psychopathology to psychology. At this time a quarter century ago when Vladimír was writing his diary at night, he was living in a room adjacent to mine, a space that had been a smithy, and I, too, was just breaking through into another realm with my writing and understanding — roughly speaking, I was moving beyond psychic automatism through realism, through a return to lived experience. So at this time Vladimír and I would stand in the doorway between our rooms and yell at each other, each dumping a bucket of swill on the other, each whacking the other across the face with the livers and guts we had ripped out of one another, hollering at each other through the slammed door and through the wall and across the apartment blocks from Žižkov to Libeň and back again, without ever realizing we were both talking past one another. At these times Vladimír thought it best to hide my hatchet and I lock up his kitchen knife. But it would be a mistake to think we didn't like one another! Within twenty-four hours after such psychic pogroms we were again guzzling beer together, and Vladimír was charming our fellow drinkers, and his extravagant gestures and speech even drew in those who had come across the street with pitchers to fetch beer and were standing by the tap in slippers. Then we would walk the outskirts at dusk and night and slowly return to the questions of art that were always on our minds, and as we gazed at Prague from Pražačka or from Šlosberk Hill, our eyes glittered with the reflection of the nocturnal city only to finish feasting on this vast, unfathomable view of Prague adorned with electric light in Vladimír's room . . . looking into his microscope, excited by billion-sided matter in constant motion. And my hatchet was again standing in the hall and Vladimír's kitchen knife was lying amicably on his table. At this time when Vladimír was writing his diary at night, which resembled an operating room protocol, a book where the position of the viscera are recorded, such was the life we shared at 24 The Levee of Eternity Street, in the same way his rhythmic swings between love and malice put him at odds with his classmates from art school as well as with his mother and coworkers and bosses. These shifts in his interpersonal relationships described a sinusoid, an ebb and flow, in black and white, so he madly loved and terrorized absolutely everyone he encountered, because he would much rather be taken for a crackpot than for bourgeois. The poet Egon Bondy, who was born Zbyněk Fišer, was a frequent visitor, and whenever Vladimír read to him from his diary, he would always stamp his little shoes on the floor and shout: "Fuck me Jesus! I'd have to dig up an entire town square with a finger before such an image would come to me! And he has hundreds pouring out of his sleeve just like that! My God, Vladimír! Write poetry for fucking Christ!" And Vladimír would just smile like a fool, a lock of hair falling to his brow as he giggled and glowed with happiness, because at certain moments he would be so susceptible to fawning praise he was like a child beholding a blazing Christmas tree. And because Bondy lived in the constant fear that all the pubs would be closed at evening, in the afternoon we'd already be hauling home, just in case of that eventuality, ewers and washbowls of beer. When we'd just gone out to the street and Vladimír was in a good mood, he'd hoist his foot so high that the sole of a shoe rested on the highest rung of the ladder chained to the gas lamppost. In this pose, the nearly two-meter tall Vladimír tied his shoe while Egon promenaded under his bent knee and shouted up at him: "Fuck me Jesus! Zbyněk Fišer will get a kick out this when I get the chance to tell him!" And Vladimír, so that those walking past could have their fill of the event, would let his foot linger right under the lamp. The tying of shoes ceremony was generally an evening of exceptional magnificence, the gas lamp illuminating the wavy locks of Vladimír's unkempt mane, folks stopping and rendered speechless.

For that matter, when Vladimír was in full strut he resembled a lit streetlamp, he was so slim and his face attracted the eyes of pedestrians even at a distance. At this time nearly a quarter century ago when Vladimír was writing his diary at night, he formed a small group from the apprentices he was training at the ČKD Engineering Enterprise in Vysočany and then taught them how easy and effortless it was to produce arrays and series of splotches that could then be finished into associative forms. So this group substituted for what Vladimír was unable to achieve among his friends — the forming of a clan and art community. After work they would all go to The Chestnut Tree in the Vysočany neighborhood. It defied belief how Vladimír gave of himself to those young men. Whoever would ask him something, even if just joking, Vladimír would immediately launch into an exhaustive lecture on how he creates his prints, and he would even write letters to each one with the same élan and scientific fastidiousness found in his letters to the eminent psychiatrist Professor Vondráček. And when it was time for the apprentices to go home, Vladimír would then offer himself to the denizens who sat down at his table, and with the same meticulous forbearance pontificate to the beer drinkers that while not everyone can become an artist anyone with the desire to can draw into a finished form what they see in blots. At the time Vladimír was writing his diary at night, a young joiner named Mr. Kaifr was rooming with him, and when he came home after his shift, combed his pomaded hair, lay down on his bunk, and dozed off, often I saw Vladimír kneel under the droplight, which was on even during the day because the sun never penetrated our rooms, a swath of his hair glittering in the light of the bulb like brass shavings, and hold forth on the miracle of matter and its reflection in the human mind, yet Kaifr was deep in slumber. And still, after a few months of such Explosionalist instruction, Kaifr began to work on a jewelry box for his girlfriend, applying to the lid twelve images of wood veneer, having traced with a brush the forms he saw in the smoky amorphousness. At the time Vladimír was writing his diary at night, he let his friend from art school, Bouše, live here, who was working at a dam and would return so utterly exhausted all he could do was lie down and drop off rather than nourishing himself on art as Vladimír had wished. So he brought home another friend, Pithart, a graphic artist, who worked on his prints, sheet-metal etchings, day and night, and for a printing bed he used a giant iron slab, which at different hours of the night always fell from the table and shook the entire building, even the entire street, so that every night the other tenants would wake up and run out to the courtyard balcony in their pajamas, everyone in a panic from the appalling thud. Only Vladimír laughed, elated by such abrupt awakenings, because he loved screwups and catastrophes, he even invited misfortune and always felt graced by what filled others with fear and dread. And at this time I would walk under Vladimír's windows and look in, over and over, as when I lay down I couldn't believe what I'd seen in his room so I had to get up to have another look, and nearly every time it was the same scene: Vladimír kneeling under his droplight and lecturing on Explosionalism to the sleeping Kaifr and Bouše, imploring and rhythmically wielding my hatchet, which was shimmering just like a curly lock of his fair hair. I walked under his windows and saw how his two friends were listening to him, but through some other signal system of sleep. Pithart was the only one who produced work, but it was large realist prints. Sometimes a pretty young woman in a leather coat popped in to bring Pithart food in her handbag, so in addition to the sharp hatchet, tin spoons were also in motion in the chiaroscuro of the room, while the edges of the iron slab ominously gleamed, as if they were reckoning when would be the most inconvenient time of night to fall to the floor with an appalling thud. The pretty woman in the leather coat was with the police, and she later took Pithart away because he'd lost so much weight on account of his printmaking. When he and the girl carried off the iron slab, handling it as if it were a sewing or washing machine, the entire building and neighborhood breathed a sigh of relief.

So this was generally how Vladimír lived when he was writing his diary at night, the very personification of the dogmatic creator, a synthesis of Prince Myshkin and Stavrogin, a master of horror and unbelievable humility, an artist whose creative drive, as the years rolled by, transformed everything negative into a positive. Today he would be fifty if he were still alive, and his friends, among whom he is more alive than when he was still here, are publishing from his diary "One-Seventh" with such reverence it's as if Vladimír himself had selected from his prodigious book the sections he felt were important and then publishing it as part of his Explosionalist Editions under the title *One-Seventh*. I should also add that it was Vladimír's death that opened a vista onto his life, in which he tried to bore down to the tissue and core of matter to reach its innate beauty and celebrate and spiritualize Great Mother Matter with his prints . . .

One time Vladimír, the poet Karel Marysko, and I went mushroom picking outside of Prague. In the train we joked about the relationship between marriage and the gold ring glittering on Vladimír's finger. Marysko didn't much like the ring because he thought it looked conventional. Vladimír said: "You don't like this ring?" And the poet Marysko said, "not especially." And before anyone could stop him, Vladimír removed the gold ring and tossed it from the moving train into the backdrop of the Klánovice Forest speeding past. Our jaws dropped, we were speechless, because we knew how much Vladimír loved that ring as a symbol of his love for Tekla, whom he'd just recently married. Yet Vladimír, his voice betraying no emotion, quietly explained in the silent compartment that tubercular cows get milked the most. And I know today that this ring flying backward from the moving train, this sovereign gesture, was for Vladimír an act all the more creative the more painful the loss. Besides, Vladimír dealt with everything in his life in the same way he dealt with that ring. Five years ago, on St. Nicholas Day, which he so loved that in a display of goodwill he would give away everything he had, he decided to conduct an experiment on himself, alone, unsuspecting, and given his complete lack of guile he couldn't suspect, that the final link in the causal chain would not connect to the last anticipated ring . . . and the door latch treacherously clicked . . . and the cord tightened around his neck, and tightened more . . . and this time, unlike at other times, no human hands came to the rescue . . . and Vladimír plunged head first from the levee of the present straight into the heart of eternity.

THE TENDER BARBARIAN

Vladimír, a master of tactile imagination, always dying, checking out, only so he could rise from the dead each time, rejuvenated, always gathering his strength to smash his head through the wall to get to the other side and follow the umbilical cord back to the origins of all things, back to the first week of Creation. He managed to be at once ancient as the world itself and as young as the light of dawn, like leaves just budding. Vladimír knew how to stake his continually restored, rejuvenated life, he knew how to make it precarious, subject it to trial by fire. That's why he loved pain. When it wasn't inflicted from the outside he inflicted it on himself. He felt responsible only to himself alone and to the elements that formed him. His prints returned to these elements a refined material structure . . .

He revived several myths . . . The myth of Dionysus, the drunken beauty who is the source of creativity, and the myth of Antaeus, the hero whose strength derived from his contact with the earth. Vladimír would become excited over a cement mixer and its bowels, a pot of hot tar, a jackhammer, an acetylene tank with hose and torch quietly purring and glowing blue, a metalworker's solder, a blowtorch, the white ice covering a fish counter, a housepainter and the splatters of paint on newspaper, dried come stains on his boxers, bloodstains on the sheets . . .

All the vices of the era passed through Vladimír: pettiness, histrionics, pathological petulance, hypersensitivity, playing the fool and imbecile, dogmatism, romantic melancholy and dreaminess, an aversion to neckties and a fondness for slogans and banners, playing the standard-bearer, intolerance, disdain for intellectuals, humbleness and megalomania, a penchant for obscenity, balcony gossip, hysteria, touchiness, narcissism, sentimentality, suspicion . . .

Yet Vladimír was able to do what a modern automobile does: deliver the mixture to right under the spark plugs without flooding the carburetor. Raw matter delivered right into the realm of transcendence. And this required placing great demands on the material. Vladimír possessed this ability. The pressure coefficients in his head withstood the most extreme incandescence of matter, not more and not less than Vincent van Gogh, Munch, Pollock. This is why his emotional swings were his health. Only in this way could he set the foundations of his scientific imagination, only through a subjective relationship with beloved matter could he penetrate the objective zeitgeist. His prints are the apotheosis of his materialistic worldview. Vladimír was the embodiment of the proletarian artist whose work celebrates human labor through new insights, and this linked him to all those who strive for an active love toward humankind, an active transformation of the world. That all he took from the social contract was a sense of duty, that he proved to himself alone, by experimenting on himself, that war can only be declared on yourself, that you can plunder no other territory but your own, which is in your head, his life not only demonstrated that the exploitation of humans by humans was a thing of the past, but in the name of the Explosionalist creator it abolished the class struggle as well, because living in peace can only ever be at the expense of the universe and yourself . . .

Corborundum grinding wheels, their sparkling tail removing rust and defects from steel rods, represented for Vladimír a heuristic symbol for both the individual and society as a whole. For half a year I worked the pendulum wheels at the Poldinka steel mill, and whenever Vladimír came to the shop floor where ten wheels hung from chains and were operated by ten goggled grinders, he was always so moved that he stared wide-eyed, each time marveling at what he was seeing and imagining . . .

One day Vladimír and I were leaving Krofts', the pub old-timers still called Pudils', having an animated discussion, when we walked past a baby carriage abandoned on the sidewalk with a crying infant inside. Vladimír froze. He analyzed the child's crying, hopped back to the stroller, and lifted up a still smoldering cigarette butt from the infant's swaddled head, theatrically displaying the odious insect before stamping it out. Someone had tossed a lit cigarette butt from an open window. Another time as we were stepping out he said: "Doctor, you'll buy me some paper and inks, won't you? If you do, you know what, inspired by that child in the stroller and the burning cigarette by his little ear I'll make a print for you. A fantastic print, only for you, about that infant. But you're not going to buy me any paper and ink, are you . . . ?"

Vladimír, Bondy, and I so loved beer that when the first ones arrived at our table we would terrify the entire pub by scooping the foam in our hands and smearing it on our faces and rubbing it into our hair like Jews rubbing sugar water on their *payot*. When the second round was brought, we repeated the foam ritual and glittered and smelled of beer for miles around. But we were just fooling around, just expressing our passion for beer, reveling in youthful enthusiasm.

We were brash beer dudes . . .

Vladimír would traverse Prague at such a brisk pace that he reduced the distance between Žižkov and Libeň, between Košíře and Střešovice. The afternoon of the day he tossed his wedding ring into the Klánovice Forest from a moving train, we lost him in the woods around Kersko. The next morning when I opened the door to my Libeň apartment a small note fell out that said: "I reached Prague via Český Brod in 12 hours. I'll tell you all about it. Best, Vladimír." So this is how Vladimír popped up in Hlubočepy, popped up in Medník at his Surrealist friends. And when he had an exhibition somewhere he would take the train the night before the opening so he could savor all the minutiae of the exhibition and during the opening, things that never happened . . . Vladimír was interested in things that could've happened. He taught the Explosionalist method of drawing to a friend who had at home several cubic meters of argillite animal fossils. Vladimír liked to draw theses imprints of fossilized crabs into human portraits, and when this friend invited him to go fossil hunting in the Koněprusy caves, he said: "No way,

I've shown you how to make active prints and told you more than anyone else. Since you're so familiar with these caves I'm afraid you'll bump into me and knock me over into some chasm and then you'll pass off my ideas as your own . . . no way. Go on your own . . ."

Vladimír hated money. As soon as he received the first installment of his monthly pay he spent it so he could borrow ten, twenty crowns a day against the second installment, scrupulously writing the names of his creditors on his locker, and when he got it he would reliably settle up, standing there and handing out what was owed to each person. Then he stood with the remainder in his hand and cackled: "What should I do with this? Toss it into the stove or spend it?" So he spent the remainder of his pay and felt good about it when that night he had to borrow sixty hellers for tram fare or cigarettes and then walked home. Receiving several thousand crowns for illustrating a book mortified him . . . His mother got two thousand, his mother-in-law another two, and several hundred he spent at once, and when his mother, convinced Vladimír had money, left to give him a taste of what a home without a mother was like, he manically spent any money he had left over and was relieved that once again he had to borrow sixty hellers for the tram. At this time we, too, thought Vladimír had enough to live on for several weeks. When I went to visit him, the neighbor opened her door and quietly told me when I remarked that for the time being at least he's living well: "Don't think so, last night he ate the potatoes I left in the hall . . ."

At this time we would argue with such vigor, as there was always a good reason for us to argue, that when the neighbors chided Vladimír he defended himself by saying: "Me? He's the problem, not me!" And he pointed at my window. And when they chided me, I would say: "Me? He's the problem, not me!" and I pointed at Vladimír's window. And once when an argument had peaked and each of us was sleeping in his room, Vladimír with my hatchet in his bed and me with his kitchen knife, and when one of us moved the other would also move, when one stood up, the other did as well, we switched on the lights and each of us showed through the doorway connecting our rooms that we had each other's weapon. So we decided to brick up the doorway. A hoary mason from Bratrská Street came by, and we took off the door and the mason covered the doorframe with tarpaper and we wrote our landlady a promise that everything would be returned to its original condition when we moved out . . . and the mason laid the bricks, scooping mortar from the wheelbarrow, Vladimír and I each sat at our own table and watched, shattered, as the bricks gradually rose higher, as a wall separating us took shape, like water rising, only the bust of the other still visible. Because Vladimír was so tall he was still sitting, and I saw only his head, then we both got up, the mason standing between us on an overturned trough, we handing him bricks, one then the other contributing to the barrier between us, the separation from table and bed, like that old crone who brought a bundle of kindling to Jan Hus burning at the stake, then we no longer could see each other, but in our undiminished zeal we still furiously handed bricks to the mason, who had calculated so accurately that the last layer of mortar matched the exact number of bricks he had brought with him . . . And when the mortar dried we sort of propped up the door . . . and breathed a sigh of satisfaction that each had created the illusion of peace from the other as each sat in the depths of his own room. Egon Bondy stopped by when the bricks were about waist-high, and he ran into my room from the hall and then right away into Vladimír's room, holding his chin, searching for the key to understand this barrier when we were still able to enter each other's room via the hallway . . . "Holy hell, what the fuck is going on here?" he brayed and ran out to the courtyard where the sun was casting hectoliters of pale lager onto the ground. When he stood in the sun Egon looked much like a faun emerging from a cistern of beer, his fair hair flowing as always down around his ears and even his beard bathed in the lager sunlight. He stood there with his hands flapping while he yelled: "Panie Wladimirze! Is it not enough for you that a wall divides Europe, that Korea is divided, that Berlin is divided and separated? You don't give a flying fuck!" And all worked up he again came into my room to look at Vladimír's head, then ran over to Vladimír's to look at my head and relish the moment when we would no longer be able to see each other, the final brick laid, the last trowel of mortar spread . . . And then in the evening when

Vladimír came home and began to write his diary, I heard his pen quietly yet vigorously bearing down on the pages of that big book of his even more so than when no wall had divided us . . . And when Vladimír tossed and turned in his bed, it was as if he were right beside me, and when he breathed, I heard it, even the swelling of his lungs, the working of his liver, I heard his heart through the wall even louder and more resonantly than when no wall had divided us. We met only in the hallway, and were civil, so that when each of us locked the door to his lair we could savor the presence of the other on the other side more than before. I pushed my bed to right against the wall, and the next day I could see from the courtyard that on his side Vladimír had also pushed his bed against the wall, so we slept like Siamese twins joined at the spine of the wall, which rather than dividing us had more closely connected us than when the door swung freely in its frame. "Are you sleeping?" Vladimír whispered. "Not yet," I whispered to the wall. "Me neither . . . ," Vladimír whispered. Sometimes we didn't speak to each other at all, but it was enough to tap the wall with a fingernail and from the other side I would hear Vladimír, just like he would hear me, scraping his fingernail against the plaster, lightly tracing lines, signaling that in reality we were greater friends than before . . . So when Vladimír later moved to the Žižkov district and would occasionally come to visit me or I go to see him at The Tram Stop, the pub across from the factory, once we got going . . . we were again friends for life, but without yelling at each other because we each had gone our own way and weren't competing with one another. So on his side Vladimír set his chair by the wall and on my side I did the same with my footstool, and we chipped and chiseled away the dry plaster, the mortar, and loosened one brick, then another, and we were all pumped up, as if each were witnessing an operation on the other, as if the chest were being opened . . . and we marveled at the beauty of the other's little room, even though no more was visible of the other than the chin or brow and a dreary white wall in the background . . . we removed several bricks, then we could see each other from the chest up, and Vladimír placed an unfinished bottle of griotte liqueur on the low wall and from the other side I topped it up with rum, shook it, and poured us drinks . . .

when we'd drunk a toast, Egon Bondy showed up and was flabbergasted . . . he stood on the footstool and looked at Vladimír, then ran down the hall into Vladimír's room from where he looked at me, at the low wall in the door frame, now a table of sorts . . . and I brought him a glass and poured him the concoction, Egon drank it down but then spluttered as if he'd drunk acid . . . he then stood by the wall, beating his little fists against the plaster, lightly banging his forehead against it, and he did the same in Vladimír's room, and exclaimed through his coughing: "Fuck me Jesus! Détente! Mutual understanding between nations has begun right here and now! I'm going to consult with the philosopher Zbyněk Fišer. A rose by any other name is still a rose! First the slap then the cuddling . . ."

Though Vladimír liked to go out bareheaded, during inclement weather he would have a black rabbi's fedora cocked on his head with the terrific elegance of a Brummellesque dandy, and when it got cold, he made a fantastical fur cap from his mother's muff, the kind one sees around nowadays, with a giant visor, a hat the rabbis of Nikolsburg might wear. When on occasion he had a tie on, one could see right off it was less a tie than a collar, or not a collar but a kind of straw band he purposely wore shifted to the left, so that the knot was half-covered by the shirt collar. He might dream of having a tony sweater and suit, but he would snap out of it and immediately declare himself a cretin, an imbecile, a moron . . .

We liked to drink beer in the World Cafeteria while watching the charladies. One had appeared in light opera in her youth, and now she was a made-up seventy-year-old decked out in a gaudy pinafore. Dancing with the broom as she swept, each man tenderly slapped her palm when she sidled up to him. A youthful comedienne. She laughed and took sips of the customers' beers, merrily singing music-hall ditties as she pushed the cart with plates of leftover food and dirty utensils. A ludicrous, batty old bag . . . Careful now! Vladimír: "She's a saint . . ." The second charlady, also a longtime retiree, once acted in tragedies for private audiences, her yellow tragic mask trampled by carnival. She sighed as she swept, as if she were raking up the remains of her own cremation. When she pushed the cart of dirty dishes she was taking her old bones to the scrapyard. Tragic twinges of conscience.

Careful now! She liked to drink, anything. Her pension was always drunk up in advance via the pails of beer she tragically went to fetch at Vaništas'. Vladimír: "Another saint . . . !" So we stood and drank and watched these two saints, a zephyr closing the door whenever someone entered, slowly at first and then a loud bang, as if behind each customer the lid of a lead coffin had slammed shut. Suddenly Egon Bondy came in: "Where've you been? I've looked in six pubs for you," he shouted and raised his arms in the doorframe, and behind him, bang! Zephyr again closing the door. Egon stuck his fingers in his ears. "Does it always do that?" Vladimír: "No, only when someone comes in . . . Mrs. Vlaštovková, do you have a screwdriver?" And Vladimír brought his chair up, put on his glasses, tightened a screw three times, and everyone waited for the next customer to walk in . . . The door closed softly, only the tragic charlady flinched, as if her spinal cord were twitching. Egon Bondy drank one beer after another, looking around at nowhere in particular. "What're you doing here?" he asked. Vladimír: "We're on a stakeout . . ." Bondy had beer running into his beard, so while another was being poured for him he sucked the beer from his whiskers. And from Upper Libeň, down Primátorská Street, came an ambulance with its siren wailing and blue light flashing in front. The tragic charlady clutched at her heart, the ambulance turned, nearly flipping over, in front of the World Cafeteria. Two old ladies in the passageway put their hands to their throats and exclaimed: "My God! Who have they come for this time!" Egon Bondy gave a start: "Fuck me Jesus, good thing nothing's wrong with me!" and he checked his pulse. Two attendants jumped out of the ambulance, pulled out a white, plastic covered gurney, then two canisters each, and they ran into the taproom and ordered the cans filled with Pilsner . . . each drank a beer for the road, and drank from glasses what could no longer fit in the overflowing cans; the two old ladies in the passageway who had taken fright wiped each other with a cloth, and the attendants with the canisters of beer ran out, their smocks fluttering, jumped into the ambulance, having first shoved in the gurney with plastic cover carting the beer, and again the siren wailed and the light began to flash and the vehicle nearly flipped over as it went into a turn, and the folks leaving Libeň Chateau clutched at their heart — who have they taken away this time? Egon Bondy said: "Holy shit, a *memento mori!* Damn Vladimír, you're a real freak magnet, aren't you?" And Vladimír was now all fired up as Egon watched a Zündapp pull up in front of the cinema, the rider clad head to toe in leather, helmeted, lugubrious as a frogman, a giant mountaineer's rucksack on his back, and he leaned the motorcycle against the curb and solemnly walked into the passage and then into the cinema. "What the holy fuck is that?" spluttered Egon. Vladimír: "It's his job, he shuttles between movie houses with newsreels in his backpack." Then we saw the helmeted motorcyclist start up his Zündapp again and carry off a newsreel to a cinema that was showing a film half an hour later, and we drank one beer after another. As we were walking away from below the chateau, the tram-stop traffic island was already lit up, the No. 13 came, a woman with a baby carriage was getting into the last car, someone was helping her, but the conductor prematurely closed the doors and the woman was holding onto the stroller now pinched in two, and as the tram took off the woman was still holding onto the handle and running with the tram, comically hopping sideways and shouting, but the tram didn't stop and the baby carriage collided with a streetlight, and crack, it broke in two, people waiting for the next tram screamed or leaned against the low wall of the chateau, a few brave souls ran toward the baby carriage. Egon Bondy turned pale . . . but bottles of beer spilled out of the broken stroller and crashed onto the ground and the aroma of spilled beer wafted over the street . . . and the woman shouted at the tram driving away: "You bastards owe me for these twenty beers! Gentlemen!" she pointed at Vladimír and Egon, "you're my witnesses. Will you testify on my behalf?" Egon Bondy thundered: "Bottles! Bottles! What about your child? Bones were shattered!" And the woman said: "That was a crate shattering. Surely you don't expect an old lady to lug around twenty beers in her arms!" Vladimír radiated bliss and creative serenity. Egon Bondy lurched into the dark of the small park, waving his arms as if warding off a bad dream: "Holy shit, this is total slapstick not even Chaplin could think up . . ."

When someone was pushing a full cart, Vladimír lent a helping hand, not so much out of an active love for his fellowman but to feel the chain on his palm, when someone was storing coal, Vladimír would offer to help. No one was ever as ardent, save perhaps two lovers hip-to-hip, as Vladimír when he had an opportunity to hold and savor in his hand a shovel's shaft, the greasy matter of a bucket handle, and he never wore a protective mask from coal dust and soot, leaving instead dark smudges of dust around his nostrils afterward . . . One day we were walking below Koráb and were struck dumb. The once barren hillside was now geometrically divided into little plots, future vegetable gardens, orchards, and folks were already pulling up weeds and turning over dirt with spades, the more sedulous even working at night and already had strawberries and vegetables in the ground. Vladimír as always picked out the plot that had been worked the least and pitched in, contending with the weeds, his whole body thrown into the work, and he liked to narrate in real time what he was experiencing as he dug up the dirt, this deflowering of maiden earth with a spade always bringing him tactile pleasure . . . At that moment we were assisting a woman who had an infant bawling incessantly in a stroller, the hillside scorching hot . . . Vladimír let the sun beat on his blond curls, and the woman kept having to tend to her child, sometimes pulling out a breast to feed her . . . At dusk, when Vladimír was about to leave he promised to come back the next day, and the woman thought Christ himself was again walking the land, so she kissed the back of his hand . . . But at another time when Vladimír was storing coal in a little courtyard shed for an elderly pensioner, he launched into a harangue about all his assorted problems and his work, and as the old lady became increasingly uneasy she took a long look at the axe wedged in the chopping block, then in desperation undid her apron and placed it over the axe . . . she sighed with relief once we left and even ran out to see if we were truly gone and had actually turned in the direction of Hausmans' . . .

Cream is made from milk skimmed from the top, diamonds from coal dust, a phoenix from a sparrow, a runner from a cripple, wherever something was insignificant Vladimír employed his talent to demonstrate *omnia ubique* and that the minimum is the maximum, that each point on the globe is the center of paradise, while hanging gardens eventually turn into ruins and dust, a dust in which all beauty endures, specks of dirt in which everything begins anew . . .

A pretty waitress worked at The Old Post Office, she sort of looked like a chubby Gypsy girl, and Vladimír liked to sit there and write letters, ever the freak magnet. When I joined him at his table a handsome young guy was in the middle of recounting his life: "When I met her my arm was in a cast so I had to hug her with this mitt and she was always moaning but got used to it. The boys drew all sorts of stuff on the cast. One writer came to the hospital for a talk and I didn't have his book so he signed my cast . . . but then everything got fucked up, my cast came off and my girlfriend said I wasn't as affectionate to her as before, even though we were about to get married . . . and she left me. Yesterday I nearly fell over! Who did I see? My ex carrying on with a guy with a cast on the same arm. These gals are all perverse" . . . Vladimír continued to write and his voice growled in indignation: "Mine also left me, so I'm writing the public prosecutor, the presiding judge of the court suggested I go easy on her . . . this is the sixth love letter I'm writing to her . . . but look, son, do you know about the Martonová experiments? I'm participating in them now. Buck naked. A nudie film. Little wires around me and my genitals, an instrument in my penis. A porno film. Little bulbs light up, the instrument's needles start to oscillate and draw lines. Data for the psychiatrist. For that Martonová, she's a doctor, you see. These instruments revealed an Oedipus complex in me. When my mother gets up in the morning I'm lurking as if by accident, just walking around naked. She still has a fine figure. She pretends not to notice me . . ." The young guy was lost in thought, his chin enveloped by the palms of his hands, his fingers all the way up to his eyes. Then he said with deliberation: "I'm paying up, you know, that girl probably takes after her dad, he's from the Podkrkonoší region. One time he took his driver's license and identity card and went to the town council to register a new trade: Anton Hulík, God. It was a month before they picked him up at the train station wearing only a T-shirt in the freezing cold. And in the nuthouse they didn't give him electroshock but something called 'vomit therapy.' They injected him with something and he would throw up for a long time, and after three months he was totally spent, and after five months he was a normal person again, a plumber, and he was given back his driver's license and identity card . . ." He got up, ceremoniously rapped his knuckles on the tablecloth, and left. Vladimír was furiously writing, streaks of vermouth glittered around his mouth, without fail the barman was bringing him his third glass, oh, what a letter this was going to be, what a letter, for clemency, on the fourth page now and Vladimír was still ascending the hill, had yet to start his descent, still in the grips of a mania where he'll say something he'll regret tomorrow . . . I left him to his writing, feeling more like taking a walk around Šlosberk Hill. My former doctor from the district clinic, now retired, had his hands out and palms up to lure titmice to sit in them and peck at nuts. Upon spotting me he addressed me as well: "And you're looking better, no autopsy required I see . . . pipipipi! So have you changed your reading habits, maybe to something a little more cheerful? Maybe humor magazines? The hare was strangled here yesterday. So where is my crested tit, my blue tit today? Tell me, is it still suppurating, is it? Well, that's fine, and your stool, has that been sorted out? It has. Well that's wonderful, a great success of science . . ." I turned so the doctor could see me better, he looked me over and continued in the same tone: "Children also feed birds from their palms, but sometimes they snatch them. Children can't be trusted. But you know, that bottle of kirsch you gave me, my wife and I drank it under the tree, we drained it. Pipipipi, where oh where is my blue tit, my nuthatch? . . . What time is it? Yes, hooligans strangled the hare we'd been coming here to feed for ten years . . ." He leaned toward me, holding my hand tight in his claws, and whispered: "You're still not entertaining thoughts of suicide are you . . . ?" I replied: "That's not me, that's Vladimír . . ." And he said, word for word: "You are Vladimír . . . Pipipipi, where oh where is my blue tit today? My nuthatch? Pipipi . . ."

Vladimír let himself be persuaded by friends to go look for motifs in nature, in the world of appearances. Two days later he showed up with easel and paint box but no paintings, and haggard, low on sleep, in a daze. "Doctor, lay off this nature stuff! We were painting the woods around Kladno. We'd just painted a landscape scene and the police showed up and arrested us for espionage. They were screaming at us till morning, demanding to know who'd commissioned the painting, on account of the other side of those little woods, where the trees thin out so that with just a slight bit of imagination you can make out the Kladno steelworks, and if our enemies were to get hold of this, they'd have a precise blueprint of its location. Beyond the woods! And so we're spies! Doctor, I would much rather paint at the expense of the universe, I'd rather be a spy of the empyrean . . ." A year later he let Rotbauer talk him into painting in the Prague suburbs. So they painted the inlet of the Vltava from Libeň Bridge. That afternoon Egon Bondy stopped by The Levee of Eternity looking for Vladimír as he had the idea that the three of us could walk upstream along Rokytka Creek at dusk and stop somewhere to drink and sing folk songs, including Vladimír's favorite, "Falcon Perched in a Maple" . . . I told him where Vladimír might be, so off we went to find him. And boom! Amid the crowd streaming down the main avenue I spotted Vladimír's head, and not alone but accompanied by the police with Rotbauer in tow, a pensioner hopping around behind them and screaming: "Good people! We have saboteurs and spies in our midst!" Vladimír was smiling, carrying his pochade box, while the police carried both paintings, and we marched behind them to Božena Němcová Street, then to Rosenberg Street, where we waited. Three hours later, sitting in the World Cafeteria drinking Pilsner, we saw Vladimír and Rotbauer walk out the door of the police station. Then over beer Vladimír related what happened: "That old retiree set the police on us because he claimed the bend in the river we were painting was a dockyard and so a vitally important area for national security . . . And when we showed them we were only interested in the trees, they hauled us in . . . So I said we were paid in dollars, and they wrote up a report! We'll just have to go back to human abstractions . . ." Egon Bondy fulminated: "Holy shit, Vladimír, you have more luck than sense. The secret police are camped out at my door and nobody even knows it! But you, they parade you in the flesh down a street swarming with folks. Fuck me Jesus! I suppose I should be jealous of all the notoriety you've achieved. Paid in dollars!"

Vladimír enjoyed taking long tram rides, until the moment the conductress punched dozens of tickets in advance. He closed his eyes, put his hand to his gall-bladder, and experienced multiple levels and different phases simultaneously . . . First, the tangible feeling of being those tickets stacked one on top the other and being perforated, then he felt a biliary colic as his liver being perforated by the punch of a gallstone, then he felt the perforation of his duodenum . . . and when he opened his eyes, he was walking and thinking about how and where he would perforate an etching, the prelude for which was the trauma experienced in the tram. His sensitivity was so acute that he enjoyed telling about dreading the moment when the tailor, making a new suit for him, knelt down and began to take his measurements . . . the moment the tailor lightly and delicately put his finger holding the tape in his crotch to measure the inseam . . . and how this ritual at the tailor's made him faint. Whenever a plane crash occurred, Vladimír wanted to know all the details. He experienced the catastrophe as if he were a passenger spilling out into space or burning up with the others on impact or blasted to pieces when the engines exploded, but mostly he experienced himself as the airplane itself plummeting into the ocean or crashing into the earth or breaking apart in the air, piece by piece falling into the countryside in accordance with its mass. When he heard about the insurance company collecting all the pieces and sticking them back together to assemble the original airplane in order to determine if there had been any foul play, Vladimír exulted: "This is like me, I'm always sticking the pieces of myself together once a week . . ."

Vladimír knew how to put himself in a state of pathological derangement so that he could then explode and discharge the sickness through his prints. He fluctuated between being morbidly ill and in rude health . . . so if you ran into him he would be in either one of these two states. Yet like nature, so Vladimír, because nature preceded him, or it could be said that Vladimír was its disciple, its product, its devotee . . . One time Vladimír and I took a trip to the Brdy forest to pick mushrooms. Actually, we went there not so much for the mushrooms as to ride the same tracks Egon Bondy lay on while waiting to be run over, narcotized by opiates to deaden the pain, but that night there was a detour from where he lay, so in the morning Egon woke up not in the realm of ontology but still on those same tracks while trains were running along different tracks. When we got to Smíchov Station we still had some time to kill, so we walked down the platform and delightedly dallied with a locomotive. The engineer was cleaning the condenser unit, and I said: "Mr. Kopic, if we passed you the ball in a lane, would you still be able to crush a goal?" And Mr. Kopic, the train engineer, formerly center-forward for Polaban Nymburk, said proudly: "You know it! Believe you me, I'd still love to strike it. And who might you be?" I said: "A fan of yours from Nymburk, from the brewery." And while Vladimír marveled, Mr. Kopic said: "Gentlemen, it's departure time, may I?" He made a noble gesture and invited us onto the locomotive. We mounted the engine, and Mr. Kopic waited until the flagman gave the signal, then he tugged on the throttle and the train started to move. During the ride Mr. Kopic told us about a father who pulled his son with him onto the tracks outside of Smíchov so that both would be run over, how he saw the son resisting but the father was stronger, like Abraham preparing to sacrifice Isaac, only God did not intervene at the last moment while peace-loving Mr. Kopic braked yet still ran over the father and son — their wriggling legs all he saw . . . Vladimír was so moved his eyes welled up. When the cloud of calamity had passed, Vladimír asked if he could hold the throttle for a moment. Mr. Kopic said he could. And Vladimír took hold of the throttle and looked through the window, then he returned the throttle and declared: "You can tangibly feel the whole locomotive in it! The whole train! The whole track." I said: "Here's the spot where Egon Bondy lay on the tracks," and I pointed, and Vladimír chimed in: "These past few minutes have been Apollinaire's 'Zone.'" Legs astride, he stood there in bliss . . . And I, who was relishing the vibrating of the entire locomotive as we rode, its shaking every time the wheels rolled over the rails, all of it registered by the whole of my body, because during the war I was a flagman, I was in the railway service, I had to ride locomotives so that I could recognize by their movement if any rail joints were defective, and compile a report correctly so the railbed could be repaired . . . I saw how for Vladimír the ride was a tactile experience not only of the machine, but also of the rails and the whole movement of the train, and again he was goggle-eyed, and I saw how at that moment he truly became the train, the locomotive, and the entire track, and how the locomotive gently and brutally engendered and kindled an amorous liaison with its tender to the extent allowed by the coupling — Vladimír froze stiff and whispered to me: "I have a hellacious hard-on." The train stopped at the village of Zadní Třebaň, Mr. Kopic wiped his hands with a cotton rag and was apologetic as he said goodbye to us: "You know, Vojta Hulík always kept his locomotive so clean he wore white gloves . . ."

Vladimír generally worked in the buff when making prints. For one, he loved being naked, and above all he approached the etching press or the copper plate exactly as if he were making love. As he gradually put himself in a state of erotic, and therefore creative, arousal, he would calculate the time between the scratching and biting of the plate so that it would span the same magnificent arc between erection and ejaculation. He always anointed his prints with semen when rolling them through the press, all his prints were mottled with this delicate carnal viscosity . . .

One time Vladimír and I took a trip up to Mělník to drink the local Ludmila wine. In the cathedral's crypt, Vladimír admired the ossuary and two skulls with cranial bone eaten away by syphilis. Afterward he was euphoric over the confluence of the Vltava and Elbe, because the Vltava was mightier than the Elbe even though the river was called the Elbe from Mělník to the sea, and that it should've been called the Vltava was something he found immensely gratifying. Afterward we walked to the village of Beřkovice, following the wall of the madhouse until evening, and Vladimír was so taken with the asylum he wished he could live there one day . . . Then on to Liběchov, where Vladimír discovered a headless statue under a leafy tree by a creek, despite it now being dark, and this put us in communication with another headless statue by Rokytka Creek. After the Ludmila wine we slaked our thirst with beer and at night walked up the stations of the cross to the ruined church. The moon glowed as we stepped from the deep shadows of a leafy alley of trees into the chalky moonlight. A stiff breeze was blowing on the church hill, and we lay down in a secluded spot and contemplated the countryside, the asylum in Beřkovice glittering brilliantly. Vladimír touched the doors and they quietly opened. We went into the demolished little church, where the moon shone through a hole in the wall. Three sheathed banners lay by the benches. Vladimír made a bed by the altar and lay down, placing a brick under his head. I lay down next to him, and because I didn't have anything to put under my head he gave me his brick and nestled his head on a bent arm. The moon dazzled as its light shone into the church. Vladimír stepped down from the altar to get one of the banners and we covered ourselves. He then stretched out his legs, the tips of his shoes tapped the unlit eternal light and set in motion its decorative receptacle hanging by three dappled chains that blazed in brilliance when it swung into the chalky moonlight . . . the pendulum of eternity disappeared into the dark like a nocturnal bird, and when it reappeared in the moonlight the receptacle blazed up like a golden pheasant, like a phoenix, its motion suspended for a moment at the apex before returning to the dark by the force of gravity and the natural movement of Vladimír's shoes. Attached by chains to the ceiling, the entire mechanism gently creaked as the rusted rings grated against one another like the discs of a diseased spine. The whole night Vladimír kept his eyes open, gazing at the unlit eternal light in motion, not blinking as we lay there supine like the Přemyslid kings with their wives . . . At daybreak, when there was enough light to see, Vladimír fell asleep with a beatific smile on his face. The processional banner draped across his chest, in the light I could see the torso of St. Wenceslas lying on Vladimír and on me the silver and gold threads embroidering the legs of the saint, who was fond of drink, liked to converse with wild animals, and was stabbed to death by his brother, because no one in the whole world will ever forgive you for wanting to live in peace and at the expense of drunkenness, and thus of the universe . . .

Agony and ecstasy were one and the same door for Vladimír, through which he could enter or exit, because for him to enter meant death and to exit life. He was not a prankster, so he wasn't one to turn things upside down, but what was already upside down he righted. So for Vladimír to be born was to die, and to die was to be born. This is why he was prone to stigmata, not in the sense of wounds opened in honor of Christ, but that he was riddled with stigmata from metalwork and his Vulcanian métier's means of expression, his arms and legs a mass of scars. He so loved his factory that if he could've lifted the bar of his hysteria just a little higher, brass filings would've spilled from his fingers, he would've coughed up fine shavings and spat out steel dust . . . As for iron and sulfur, manganese and carbon, lime and water and the other minerals nature has marshaled to construct the human body, when the same such minerals and metals came close to Vladimír's body, all of these elements rejoiced and beckoned and he only had to observe their desire and love for their kindred metals, which having died were rising from the dead, swirling in the realm of metamorphoses . . .

When I returned from Paris, I had to brief Vladimír for several hours on everything I'd seen. He was enthralled: "About this Paris, Doctor, it must be magnificent, almost like Libeň, maybe somewhat like Vysočany, and if I really let my imagination run wild, Paris's beauty rivals Žižkov's. What you've told me has reignited my love for Utrillo, with his walls, those flaking walls he managed to paint so beautifully that just a glimpse of them will make you want to pull out your cock and piss on them. Like I say, Doctor, that Paris must be magnificent . . ."

Vladimír took a ritual, sacral approach to everything. He always arrived at work a half-hour early so that bit by bit he could prepare himself, like a priest for Mass. When he received a letter, first he was incredulous, then picked it up again and carefully reread the address. When he was satisfied it was indeed for him, he put it on the table, then he meticulously washed his hands and carefully opened the letter. Then he walked around, and only when he sat down and put on his glasses did he read it, slowly, then he folded the letter back up and reread it one more time later. And after that he placed the letter in a valise with hundreds of other letters, with thousands of other writings. He adopted the same approach when he wrote a letter, an act he never took lightly. First he would jot down an entry in his diary, then he would go off somewhere to be alone, preferably a pub, where he would order a beer, supplemented with a vermouth, and if the letter should be more strident than usual, he would have another vermouth. When he finally felt himself to be in a state of grace, he began to write, furiously, his manner of writing like turning on a spigot. When he finished, he would ceremoniously light a cigarette and reflect on the letter and evaluate what sort of reaction it would produce, and if he felt it would cause outrage, he ordered another vermouth to give him the courage to lick the envelope and toss it into the mailbox. He always drummed his fingers atop the mailbox and felt around in the slot with a finger to see if the letter could be retrieved. The next day he would be reckoning if the letter had already arrived and mentally relishing via the eyes and mind of the recipient how much offense, pain, or even delight it produced. Vladimír's letters were always personal and aggressive. The more he thought a letter might offend, the more healthy he felt. When he was planning to visit someone, he always took the entire afternoon to prepare, fastidiously bathing, shaving, and inspecting himself in the mirror to see what suit or sweater looked best on him. When he climbed the stairs or entered a house where he was expected, envisioning the encounter made him lightheaded, dying at the thought of what he would say . . . He always prepared for any meeting, regardless with whom, as if it were a tryst with a woman who might conceivably or likely have him undress. He approached his work in the same way. He was always perfectly prepared, having thought out in advance what to wear or to work in the nude. Each session with the etching press was a Mass, a ceremonial procession, a symposium. Catholic ritual pervaded Vladimír subconsciously and unconsciously, and this is why each and every event with Vladimír bore the stamp of the arcane. Yet ceremony allowed him to state in company what he found objectionable about them as a group in general while also singling out certain individuals, launching his attacks with such vigor that those targeted fell off their chairs. Ceremony gave Vladimír a screen behind which he could discreetly confess all his complexes, all of his sexual and erotic obsessions, such that he could suddenly transfix people the same way a ringed python does a bunny. When in the company of others, Vladimír initially would agree with everyone, telling each they were right, then all at once he would find his strength and say: "But if you'll permit me . . ." and completely flip-flop on what he'd said a moment before, and just as if in Mass, he transubstantiated an ordinary wafer and a deciliter of white wine in his tangible body and in his blood, with which he would anoint those present, whether they wanted it or not . . .

Vladimír didn't really like dialogue. Or he did, but just in his own particular way, such as asking how to get to the train station and so forth. He understood a genuine dialectic as a method for arguing with himself, the spurs of antitheses driving him toward monologue. Monologue, this was Vladimír's cup of tea . . .

Vladimír was a magnet for the crime and local news sections of all the evening papers, yet he also always managed to remain aloof from any event he was at the moment in the thick of experiencing down to the last detail. One day we went to Klánovice, and as we were walking by the cottages and villas Vladimír became captivated by a pine tree held in place by a chain as it was being chopped down by cottagers. The pine had to fall between a cottage and the garage. The tree's tragic fate was imminent, and it loudly wailed as it was being felled by saw and axe. The trunk, chained to a capstan winch, the kind used in ports to reel in boats to the pier, was already tilting enough. Vladimír stared, getting jumpy, a workman once more cranked the lever, as it were, and then several more times, and the century-old tree was finally ready to fall and was slowly crashing to the ground, but to the horror of everyone the forked crown was going slightly askew and the tree was about to fall right on the garage and split it in two. "Oh no, no!" groaned the transfixed onlookers. Vladimír was the only one to jump to the winch and give the lever a few more cranks, and the chain restrained the tree just enough so that it fell between garage and cottage. Horror was replaced by relief. Vladimír said: "Gentlemen, I've never chopped down a pine tree in my life, but I am a toolmaker at the ČKD plant in Prague–Vysočany, and nothing more needs to be said!" Another time Vladimír and I took a trip to the village of Doubrava, which he wanted to see because it's accessed by a single road that ends behind the village at the Elbe. We rode bikes to Byšičky, which also has a single road that circles the village green, and then you have to go back, because like with Doubrava, this is the end of route and road, too, so to go forward you have to go back. And in Byšičky we witnessed this: Villagers were standing in a gateway and staring into the middle of a yard, boys were sitting on a wall staring into the middle of a yard, the heads of villagers peered over the neighboring fences and stared into the middle of a yard from where came the whine of a buzz saw. Vladimír knew at once what was likely happening in the yard. We walked in and I, rooted to the spot, gawped with the others . . . In the middle of the yard with the droning buzz saw, a man was practically genuflecting before it like a priest at Mass, with his entire head, up to the throat, embedded in the still revolving saw, which, given its oscillation, was cutting a one-centimeter wide incision into his neck and skull. The saw table was covered in blood glittering in the sunlight, the hands of the dead man lay in the drying blood, and everyone watching was transfixed, because this was such a tragic and astonishingly beautiful spectacle that it had immobilized and plastered every limb of these sentient folk. Only Vladimír jumped over to the saw and pressed the button under the table, his sleeve covered in blood when he stood up, and the saw's buzzing abated, and when it had gone silent, the spectators regained their movement, but they started to disperse as if chronic rheumatics, and only a few dared to approach the calamity, over which Vladimir's curly head bathed in light towered toward the sun. Vladimír raised his hands into the refulgent day and shouted: "Don't touch anything until the police get here. Do not touch!" And we rode back on the bikes, Vladimír's blood-soaked sleeve glittering and quickly drying in the sun, his head erect, eyes open wide, cleaving the onrushing air, for he always felt graced by fate when brought to the scene of a misfortune . . . When Egon Bondy heard about this, he examined the palms of his hands for a long time, turned red, but then got hold of himself: "I'm finished with being mad at you. I now have to reach a place where you can't get to me, where I'll be invulnerable . . . the last level of Indian philosophy where even nirvana is at a standstill . . . And because Vladimír is capable of anything, I'll kick the ladder away so you can't get to me . . . as for that road leading to Doubrava and ending in the river, that road to Byšičky circling the village green and the way forward is the same as the way back, I'll certainly go to check it out for myself . . . this is my route and road, this is the path taken by Egon Bondy . . . Fuck me Jesus! . . ."

An elderly lady named Miss Šulcová, who picked through garbage cans and dumpsters and sold old paper and rags and metal to the scrapyard, fell in love with Vladimír. She wore black gloves, and her little face was made up in vermilion, and because she didn't bathe layers of this makeup built up on her cheeks, and the layers became as flaky as the dough of a schaumrolle. She had the fixed idea that Vladimír was an Adventist minister. To get in his good graces, she would come to clean for him, and one time brought him a coat from a dead mason who'd been stabbed to death in the back, and another time she brought him a suit from someone who'd been murdered and tossed into a lime pit at a construction site. Another time she brought us an unfinished bottle of liqueur, and when we'd polished off the nasty stuff she told us she'd pulled it from a garbage can. Once she brought a modern-looking statuette of a cat or dog, but then whispered to Vladimír that an actual cat was inside, that for fun concrete masons had tossed it into wet cement and then threw it through the air and the cat stiffened and died inside its cement cuirass. But one time after Christmas Eve Miss Šulcová came over and told Vladimír she had brought some Gypsies home to her apartment, and as they went about knifing each other at night they had also wounded her in the darkness, so she was now happy to sleep in an abandoned shop, but at night hungry rats come out, and they devoured the Christmas bread Vladimír had given her, even though she had put it on her chest. So one evening at dusk, Vladimír bought a loaf of Christmas bread and marched to Kotlaska Street. We met Egon Bondy on the corner of Na Žertvách, and when he saw the Christmas bread he flapped his hand. So Vladimír told him all about Miss Šulcová, how he had cut out the fatal stab wounds from the coat, how he had stuck this on a canvas and wanted to complete the piece of cloth with painting, and then he left us by saying he wanted to sleep with Miss Šulcová so that during the night he could do battle with the rats over the Christmas bread on her chest, and he would tell us how it went in the morning, that he wasn't just going to give in to rats without a fight. Egon Bondy spread apart some thick boxthorn bushes and crawled in, only his feet peeping out, and in those bushes by the tracks he yammered: "Oyoyoyoy! Oy! The Dharma bums are in Prague! And I know nothing about it . . . Aye! Today I'm going on a serious bender with Zbyněk Fišer! Aye!"

In the World Cafeteria sat a certain tailor who observed the world only through the prism of *The Protocols of the Elders of Zion*. One day he got into an argument with Vladimír over his handwriting. Vladimír told him an analysis of his handwriting indicated that he's a loner and a melancholic. Judging from the letter *b* he should be a forester, kill his wife and bury her in the woods, and then let everyone search for her! The tailor was so taken with this vision that from the moment of the buried wife in the woods he christened Vladimír "magnificent champ!" Then a momentary interruption, a Gypsy brawl, wild gesticulations, everything on the floor. When Mrs. Vlaštovková had hauled out the brawlers and with mighty kicks sent them running across the entire square before plopping down under the Jan Podlipný monument, no damage was found, just a punched doorframe. And next to us a man was writing a letter, wetting the pencil for half an hour before putting down the line: "I sincerely extend to you both hands." After this brawl at the expense of the air and a scraped knuckle, Vladimír reminisced: "Oh, my brother and I fought all the time, and when we made up, as brothers, we would gently butt heads like billy goats. During the night an epileptic seizure left him with a fractured skull." The man licked the pencil and wrote another line: "Dear Evženie, let's not grate on each other's nerves." He was writing a letter, he was old, purple nose, a nose purpled with veins and thick as an earthworm. Worked up about the forester and the buried woman, the tailor said: "Magnificent champ, you have a nice coat. Neck six, back also six, this is in vogue in America. Let out a centimeter under the navel and take in the waist three fingers . . ." He pulled out his measuring tape, and when he commenced to measure Vladimír's pants and touched his crotch, Vladimír spilled his beer . . .

When Vladimír was getting divorced, an army officer sitting in the Out of the

Way tavern boasted: "Do what I do, take a belt to her hide!" When we ran into this officer a month later at The Tram Stop, he was all bent over, crosseyed, and in tears he said: "Come have a drink with me." He tearfully laid it all out: "My wife's kicked me out. Before she did I tried to show her how sorry I was by taking apart the typewriter, down to the last tiny screw, but she didn't understand. I'm going to hang myself, I can't sleep, and when I do it's standing up. I moved the cupboard a little so that in my misery I can sleep while standing..." But then a man showed up and opened his shirt to show us that he had a hole instead of vocal cords. He needed to open his heart, and Vladimír, it was always the Wailing Wall with him, said: "What's your name?" The man pulled out a notepad and wrote "Václav Kopecký. Over the past two years I've had 2,800 injections and 28 operations, on Monday they're stitching up the tracheostomy... my beloved wife ran off with another guy ... my nerves are shot ... she stole 500 crowns from me ... I know her name is Jarča, but others know her, if I run into her, I'll let her pick up her things..."

Mrs. Vlaštovková is tanned. Vladimír steals glances at her, at the giantess, Mrs. Vlaštovková, who's slinging mugs of freshly poured Pilsner, sending them flying across the counter right into the hands of waiting drinkers. "What am I?" asks the barmaid. Vladimír: "You are a pink piglet the color of a withering peony." And Mrs. Vlaštovková with a hearty laugh: "And what are you?" Vladimír without hesitation: "A meteorological station with steel wool for a brain." A young man has entered, scouring the joint for someone to punch in the face, a fine specimen of the pugnacious Czech, a lad relentlessly seeking justice for those who've been wronged. With no one on the horizon, he leaves with a swift kick to the door, scowling, cap low over eyes on the lookout for their objective. We go out and through the crossing gates, a bush of white roses sprawled over the control box to the gates. Vladimír: "As if someone had thrown a curtain over the box..." Deranged citizens are freely lining up for the evening daily *Večerní Praha*. Jasmine blouse. Green skirt. Vladimír: "Look, Doctor, no way you're buying any for me! I need inks the color of the Sunday edition of *Rudé právo*, a dozen of burnt sienna, two dozen of black, a dozen of vermilion, but no way you're buying them for me, are you? Also two dozen of Parisian blue, a dozen of umber, and one of white, but no way you're buying them for me, are you? Really? OK, so two more dozen on Thursday and then you'll see. And I trusted my wife so much," now venting, "that I practiced self-strangulation in front of her, to bring her a little joy. But she was at your place again. Hah! She went skinny-dipping! At noon! The fishermen cast their lines all wacky, a cyclist rode off the side straight through the weeds on the slope and gladly right into the river, so tell me, what did her body look like, tell me! Swear to it! What? In the afternoon she tossed a tampon into the toilet, I fished it out with my hands. Of course I had the right, I was her husband then . . . I miss her, Doctor, what am I without her . . . ?" And Vladimír walks back in the direction of Palmovka toward the crossing gates, crying, his eyes two gurgling water mains, his weeping so heartfelt, his sorrow borne with head held high, like a fleuron, like a flambeau, and those walking past from the opposite direction, women mostly, turn toward him, nostrils flaring, every second one desiring Vladimír . . .

When Vladimír's chest was hurting or he had rheumatism in an arm, he would always buy ordinary grain alcohol, known as pure grain, or simply as rye, and then rub it onto his chest or tennis elbow. When he had a bad sore throat, he would soak a scarf in the alcohol to make a compress for his neck, and when he had a fever, we would drink half a bottle of the rye and pour the rest onto a towel and wrap it around his chest, because this is what his grandmother did. For that matter, we knew in advance what type of alcohol we would be buying when wages were disbursed, and we knew this almost a year ahead of time as we stood in front of liquor stores and selected what we wanted, debating and arguing over which types of alcohol best suited our states of mind right then. Sometimes we bought two different types and mixed them. For example, a bottle of rum is excellent when mixed with cherry liqueur, a bottle of rum is quite tasty when mixed with green crème de menthe, we called this concoction the Cavalier, and at other times we mixed rye with rum and called it Brickwork . . . or we drank each bottle on its own, always poured into small glasses . . . so a ritual developed. We locked the bottle away in the cupboard our landlady had left us, and when we unlocked it we always ceremoniously poured shots, locked the alcohol away again, took a sniff of it, clinked glasses, and then drank it down according to our temperament, sometimes draining it in one go, sometimes in sips, singing its praises, and when we had finished drinking we wrote for awhile, but before fifteen minutes had passed we were again standing before the cupboard and unlocking it, like a priest at the high altar, and again we were pouring ourselves a shot and again drinking it down and were astonished at how little of the bottle remained, but a bottle of alcohol is like a vacation, it goes by slowly at first then over the final week the days just fall away like those shots into our ecstatic gullets, because what we always appreciated in booze was how we became ever lighter, how rapturous we became, smiling like fools, how this liquor and the ritual unlocking and locking of the cupboard bonded us for so long that we declared in unison that this final glass should not be drunk … And we each tottered off to our beds and observed how the alcohol reversed its polarity in our bowels and head, turning a splendid sleep into a listless state of mind in the morning … And we gave no one even a thimble-full from the bottles we purchased with our wages, we had other booze for them, this was our secret, every time someone stopped by we'd hide the glasses under our beds and neither one of us drank a single drop without the other, because this was solely our thing, like how I drink coffee, a ritual I've continued to this day, only able to drink coffee alone, only savor the sips of coffee alone, while smoking three strong cigarettes and thus putting myself into such a splendid meditative mood that if someone should come by I immediately put out the cigarette and don't finish drinking the coffee and let the ritual lapse the whole day — in the same way Vladimír and I would open and close that beautiful cupboard, which, when he definitively moved away from Libeň, I opened and drank on my own in his honor, yet without Vladimír it was a desecration of the Host, so I bought the cupboard from the landlady, and with the hatchet Vladimír used to hide from me I chopped it into pieces and burned them in the stove, listening to the flames hiss and lick with relish the wood saturated with liquor and memories …

Vladimír also knew how to talk to animals. Whenever he encountered a cat he immediately held out a finger, and by touching the cat's snout establish communication with it. He would say: "Doctor, whoever is friends with animals is friends with God gratis, and in one fell swoop unites the lowest with the highest and closes the circle, just like with me when a print made from all that factory refuse propels me to the most powerful metaphysical bursts. Hahaha . . . !" And so one day we were out walking above Kelerka, where there's a small pond that used to have willows like straight out of Erben's poem, and we popped into The Talking Dog, a pub that indeed had an Alsatian who was quite intelligibly telling the customers to fuck off and was even more exact in its pronunciation of "shit," and as we were returning through the Prosek cemetery, that entire sacred ground overgrown with ivy, we came to the Prosek church, and since it was open we went in, because this church was close to a thousand years old . . . a charlady was wiping the pews and a marvelous cat accompanied her, the kind of cat I'm especially fond of, a tabby with white paws and chest and pink nose, and the cat walked along the pews, and when the charlady knelt to wipe the altar, the cat leapt behind her onto the table to sit next to the bell for the elevation of the Host and survey the scene as if it were the ministrant or beadle or perhaps something even more, as Vladimír feared . . . Then the charlady finished her worked, genuflected, bowing way low, and the cat marched behind her. She locked the church and went into the parsonage with the cat in tow. When Vladimír and I attended Sunday Mass at the church, it was just as he had foreseen. During High Mass the cat sat next to the bell, looking at the altar in such a way that when we in the first row turned, we saw that no human face displayed such piety and such wisdom as did that feline, and Vladimír whispered to me that the cat, watching in delight as the priest officiated the rites, was in direct communication with God, and caroming back through the medium of the priest, God was in direct contact with the cat, so that in exceptional cases cats took precedence over those of tepid faith and heaven must be full of cats. When Egon Bondy heard this idea, he said in anguish: "I'm going to go lie down. Fuck me Jesus, where does this psychopath get this stuff? Actually, no, I'm not going to lie down, I'm just going to collapse right here, right now, call an ambulance to take me away, and not your standard one but the kind with a blue light flashing on top . . . it's going to be one hell of a night again . . . !"

One time at The Town of Rokycany Vladimír froze and stared into a corner. I looked at Vladimír and I saw that something extraordinary was happening in that corner of the pub. "Rumen," said Vladimír, "swallows in flight," he added when I still didn't understand, and his index finger wiggled his lower teeth. Without even turning around, I said, "Aha, a mother is taking hot puree from a thermos with a teaspoon and first warming it in her mouth . . ." "Or she's cooling it," Vladimír added, and I continued: "And then she's feeding her child mouth to mouth." Vladimír nodded his head and said: "No." And I shook my head no and said: "Yes." I quietly blurted: "Aha, two lovers are smooching and she's asking him to swap spit." Vladimír shook his head no and said: "Yes." Elated, I nodded yes and said: "No." Vladimír: "Doctor, promise me that if I end up like this you'll be there to do the same for me . . ." I said: "I promise," and shook my head no. Then I turned around to see what had made such an impression on him. Two friends were sitting at a table, one was conscientiously chewing while the other was waggling his lips . . . And then I saw it! The one who'd been so diligently chewing now spat masticated salami onto a plate and the other who was toothless ate it with a fork and knife as if what his friend had chewed up for him were hashed beef. "Ungelt," I said. And Vladimír was lost in thought and shook his head no, but smiling, so that I saw he was looking at a fresco of the old man receiving drink from the breast of a beautiful young woman. "Crisis situation," said Vladimír. I said: "And during the war?" Vladimír murmured: "The horror . . . you know, I'd like to try it one day?" And the local idiot, so he seemed to me, came in and over to our table, he clicked his heels and announced: "Mr. Elias, we have repainted the green fire engine red! Vladimír said: "I'm not Elias, I'm Job. This is Elias," and he pointed at me. And the glorious imbecile announced to me that they had repainted the red fire engine green . . .

Vladimír was looking through binoculars at ravens slowly flying over Libeň above Šlosberk in the direction of Chabry. He set them down and said: "Doctor, the wisest birds in the world are ravens and crows. No flying in formation, no quasi-military array in the sky, each bird just hangs around as it pleases and eventually reaches its destination. And then they are so modest. They are like a species of black Diogenes. When they descend on a field, they help themselves to budding grain, and when there is none, then the stubble, and when that's gone, then they start in on the haystacks or manure, and they're fine with it. From now on when I don my black rabbi's fedora it will be like I've set a raven on my head. I'll also buy a black turtleneck in their honor. And then they'll nest and hatch in their thousands in the treetops at Baron Chotek's chateau in Veltrusy, and since the trees at the Bohnice mental asylum are full of them in winter, the lunatics call them Bohnice hens. The old ravens, who have a nose for gunpowder, fly off when someone shows up with a rifle. And, Doctor! Doctor! Have you ever seen a raven as roadkill? I haven't — swallows, thrushes, pheasants, partridges, hares, but never a raven! Why? They have such precise radar that even though they have a slow takeoff the car's grille just misses them. If I had the brain of a raven my prints would be fucking fifty years ahead of everyone else's. Like I said, Doctor, the raven is my bird . . . !" So we walked and stopped for a beer at The Ship, Mr. Müller's place, the father of the fastest hockey player who was brought home dead from Garmisch-Partenkirchen, and no one knew how it happened. For a long time Vladimír observed Mr. Müller, who was cheerful and joking as he poured beers, as if nothing had happened. "That's the way it should be," Vladimír said in satisfaction, "like a raven," he added, yet when the ventilator had sucked up the smoke a photograph appeared on the wall of the curly-headed hockey player, bent forward as if leaning on his hockey stick, his skates gleaming like his hair, a smile as wide as the span between his skates. And a corner of the frame held a small diagonal piece of black crêpe. Mr. Müller rinsed the glasses and, gazing at the photo, said: "Every time I look at it the tears just start to flow . . ."

In Libeň, at 24 The Levee of Eternity, the rear section occupied by Vladimír and I had once been a smithy. Once. This section was built for a purpose, so no sunshine reached it, and when it was dusk or cloudy, we didn't need to have the lights on, but when the opposite buildings and façades and roofs were awash in sun, our two rooms were so dark we had to switch on the lights. And in addition to this paradox, during the greatest freeze outside it was like May or June in our rooms, and when the walls were just starting to exude the moisture of those winter months, anyone who entered our place from the warm courtyard would start shivering as if in an icebox. On the other hand, those argillite walls didn't begin until winter to give off the warmth they had accumulated in the hot summer months, so we didn't even need to heat the place. Vladimír didn't heat at all in winter, only in summer, with the onset of that summer frost. Because he was studying Leonardo da Vinci at the time and wanted to be an inventor and innovator like him, he set up what came to be known as "Vladimír's mirror system" in the windows, and it did the job rather well. Somewhere I had found, or pinched, I don't even know, maybe one day I'll remember how I ended up with them, but in short, I hauled home ten large oblong mirrors that perfectly fit on our rooms' inner sills between the windows, and so by virtue of the law of reflection the light from the courtyard banked off them onto the ceiling, which was so ablaze in those dark rooms that anyone who entered was taken aback. Vladimír hung one of the remaining mirrors on the inside of the two doors with glass paneling, which confused anyone coming in or wanting to leave, because they would see in the mirror part of the room behind them, where Vladimír had screwed two enormous mirrors from defunct restaurants onto the back walls, the whole wall covered in mirror, so that whoever looked in from the courtyard would always be startled to see either me or him double, or a multitude, while it was only the three of us. And one day when Miss Šulcová came by to clean our place for free, the lady who wanted Vladimír to be a priest and brought him the clothes off tragic fatalities given to her by orderlies at the Bulovka Hospital, she entered and set her bucket and mop down next to the door while her hand was still holding the door handle as her mind rehashed the divine message that had appeared to her in a dream the night before, and thinking about Vladimír, the mirror on the door was confusing her so much she thought the bucket reflected in it was in the hallway, and when she leaned out to get it, she loudly banged her forehead, then she saw the bucket at her feet, so she picked it up, and when she saw herself with the bucket in the giant back mirror, she walked toward the courtyard reflected in that mirror so that Vladimír had to direct her toward the door so she could begin cleaning it, but when she looked into the mirror on the door she saw the bucket below, and she leaned over to take the bucket from the mirror with her hand still groping around in the mirror like a kitten, and ultimately assuming the bucket at her feet was in the mirror she stumbled over it and banged her head again on the door, so we thought it better to empty the bucket and lead her out to the courtyard and out of the building entirely, but even then she was so disoriented that Vladimír had to accompany her all the way back to the shop where last Christmas rats had devoured at night the entire loaf of Christmas bread even though it was lying on her chest while she slept in her bed. When Egon Bondy saw "Vladimír's mirror system" and heard the story of Miss Šulcová, he exclaimed: "Aha! You're not going to sucker me! I've translated Morgenstern!" During the day he amassed so much beer that he sat on a chair, one leg crossed over the other, lecturing on Surrealism, on Dostoevsky, and agaze, he couldn't get enough of watching himself, so utterly smitten with his own image in the large mirror on the back wall he couldn't take his eyes off it, flirting with himself, only regularly lowering his eyes to immediately raise them again to savor all the more his own image, which so obviously delighted him. And so around midnight when we had gone to bed I was awakened by a sound like a leaky faucet . . . and then again, at which point I turned on the light and Egon was tranquilly pissing out the remains of the thirteenth of fifteen beers onto the carpet. I said, "Can't you go outside, you pig?" He lay down and said: "Oh right, and bang into one of these mirrors!" And he serenely drifted off to sleep again, his shoes glistening in a huge puddle of piss like two boats in a bay, and since I was furious at him, I pissed in each of his shoes. When Egon got up at 10 the next morning, we'd been at work for hours by then, he stood by the door buried in thought, looking into the mirror and stroking his chin, and suddenly, as he was gazing absently into the mirror, he saw his two shoes. "Who put them out in the hall? Fuck me Jesus! That Vladimír," he bellowed, and when he bent down to pick up the shoes he banged his forehead into the mirror. First he looked to see if Mr. Kaifr was still asleep after his night shift, then he quietly put on his shoes and tiptoed out. That afternoon I bought three kilos of cabbage and rubbed away the dried puddle of the poet's piss from the landlady's red imitation Persian carpet. And I smiled because I was especially fond of Egon Bondy, almost more than I was of Vladimír, which is saying something.

One time Vladimír and I set off for Hradové Střimelice, which had the oldest publican in Central Europe, ninety-one years old and she poured beer, recited Vítězslav Hálek, all of it by heart, and what she remembered from Gothic novels. Vladimír was fired up. She never told her most beautiful stories to anyone, only to Vladimír, how for twenty years she's had so much work she hasn't been able to go to confession, so she wrote to the priest all her sins, and when the priest came by to give her absolution, she had to receive it while on a stepladder since at that moment she was cleaning the upper windows . . . We were drinking green crème de menthe when a procession of masks passed by and from the dark tavern everything outside sparkled like a Tyrolean tablecloth stained with jams and all sorts of jellies . . . At times the face of an old lady emerged from the tavern, her dress the color of dusk, so that no matter how hard we tried we could only make out the face and under it a pint of beer . . . As we were walking down the hill later toward Čerčany and to the railroad, we saw a woman standing on a farm, but when she moved, the gate behind her was green with gray vertical stripes, and the woman was wearing a dress that was also green with stripes so that only her death mask shone against the gate. At the edge of the woods we jumped over a stream, a little stream flowing across a sandbank, fires were glowing in the distance where masked folk were singing and dancing and twitching and howling like bacchants . . . Vladimír stood rooted to the spot . . . The guy leading the procession with the club's standard was now lying on his back in the shallow stream, drunk, the water lapping over him, undulating like blinds; the cover of water rippled only a few centimeters over the supine drunkard, who was grinning, a smooth flint stone under his head, resting content-edly while the soaked standard fluttered across his chest through the water . . .

One time on our way for a beer Vladimír proposed: "My next print will be velvety. You know how it goes. You're just automatically kicking a pebble with your left then your right foot. So it's a small pile of brass filings. Fifteen seconds, I look at it. It's beautiful, Doctor! And like velvet! You know, all things considered I'm glad I'm a halfwit . . ." We turned into Skořepka Street on the way to the Konvikt. Mr. Fišer, formerly a Greco-Roman wrestler fifty years ago, now wrestling with sclerosis, was sitting on a stool in front of his building, and because Mr. Fišer only went to The Golden Tiger to drink beer, he waved at us, just as he does the whole day at anyone who walks past, and he wrung his hands: "Turn around, turn around, today we have hygiene inspection. A total catastrophe . . . !"

Once, when Vladimír and I were in the middle of one of our salacious periods, we were looking for material to include in a text paying homage to George Grosz. We skimmed the graffiti in factory and pub bathrooms and wrote down several dozen scribblings. By mistake we were in the ladies bathroom at the station in Veleslavín, but railway workers barged in on us and we bolted ourselves in a stall and so much screaming and hollering ensued that even the stationmaster came in. So we unlocked the door, and they all pounced on us like we were two pornographers and perverts and accused us of lurking in the bathroom for schoolgirls to sexually abuse. When we showed them our collection of graffiti from an assortment of bathrooms, the stationmaster rescinded the first accusation but continued to insist we were two homosexuals who'd come to the bathroom at the Veleslavín station to consummate our lust, and our collection of obscene graffiti was just a shiny object to divert attention . . . he spat in our faces first, then his underlings did the same, because among the hoi polloi homosexuality is considered exceptionally abhorrent. No sooner had we recovered from the incident and we were back to collecting, and so we found ourselves in the ladies bathroom at the Faculty of Arts of Charles University, where we'd come under the pretext of attending a lecture on revolutionary activities in Africa. We found such lovely graffiti there: "Girls, I fucked a black guy last night!" And below it in a girl's hand: "What about his cock?" "At least a kilo!" Vladimír was beside himself. He said: "I thought such lewd images only came to me, now I see they're commonplace . . ." When Egon

Bondy heard about it, he clasped his hands, lifted them over his head, and groaned: "Good God, you two skunks are stealing from me without even knowing it! I mean, I've been sweating of late over how best to formulate this: *Sex is anonymous, eros is individuated* . . . We're all in the same sexual boat but each sails under their own erotic flag . . . Fuck me Jesus! I'll have to swallow a kilo of pills again tonight just to get a little shuteye . . . !"

Vladimír was forever the naif. One time he and Tekla came to visit us in Nymburk. Tekla rode with my father in his White truck to fetch the Škoda he'd wrecked somewhere. We waited for them on the banks of the Elbe, and when the White drove up, Vladimír was so overcome with emotion he started to cry. My father was driving the truck, on which sat his Škoda 420 and in which sat Tekla, mimicking the movements of the steering wheel required to maneuver in reverse, pumping the brakes, and finally backing into the courtyard. Then she and Vladimír went down to the jetty for a swim. Mom and the schoolmaster's wife watched Vladimír through binoculars and saw them having sex under the transparent sheets of the river at 10:30 a.m. on Sunday while High Mass was being celebrated. Schoolmaster Cyril also had a look through the binoculars and said in anguish: "I just don't know, I really don't, but this generation doesn't seem to be following in the footsteps of Comenius." Afterward, when gently reproached for his performance in the river during High Mass, Vladimír heartily laughed: "I could see that I was seen, but I wanted to make your mother happy." When Egon Bondy heard about this, he covered his ears and screamed: "Fuck me Jesus! Doctor, for the love of God, enough already! Enough! Vladimír is fulfilling the Bible! 'I tell you that many will come from the east and the west, and will sit down with Abraham . . .' That Vladimír, paranoia pure and simple . . . !"

One time we were sitting in Brabec's and discussing the expansion of the universe while drinking beer commensurately with the topic. Ah, that Vladimír! He never went to the loo alone, and if he were visiting someone, he'd rather burst before taking a leak. So after five beers when we'd gone to take our first piss, two brothers sat down at our table and they chatted with so much animation, so much gusto, especially the one wearing dark glasses, who had a booming voice, each word so beautifully rounding out the semantics of the sign that we listened rapt to its resonant melody. Vladimír removed the crust from a bread roll because all his teeth were loose. But when these two new tablemates got up to take a piss, we saw that the one with the booming voice was blind. When they returned, our conversations merged and ultimately we learned that when these two brothers were kids they were romping around one day, and as they jumped from a tree one of them let go of some branches that flew back and lashed out the other's eyes. Standing on the traffic island as he was cadging sixty hellers from me for fare, Vladimír said: "One day when I work up the courage, I'm going to ask that blind guy if when his eyes were lashed out if by chance they turned and in that final second for the first and last time gaze into their own face, into empty sockets . . ." The next day we were sitting in The Slavic Linden in Vysočany and Vladimír was moaning about going blind, that under an eyebrow by his temple his trigeminal nerve was being pinched, and if he were to sneeze with enough force his front teeth would fly out, when he saw a tram out the window, and he groaned and gripped his right side, and when he saw the conductress in the tram punching a book of tickets, pain shot through his gallbladder, and he held his head in his hands and fingered it, prophesied a storm, a common five-inch nail embedded in his skull so that its tip touched his tongue. What's more, two days earlier he'd challenged the apprentices to a contest who could leap from a standing position onto the workbench where a steel slab lay. Vladimír won, but shredded his tibia on a corner of the slab, and it was festering, so he alternated between clutching his tibia, his side, pressing a finger on his trigeminal nerve, and wiggling his front teeth to convince himself they were way too loose. At this moment a man stood up from a neighboring table, and while keeping an eye on the wall clock quietly said: "My name is Sol, like soul, repeat over and over 'stay calm, stay calm, stay calm' . . . If you would ever need someone to perform the movement techniques of animal magnetism, I live in Horní Počernice. Ask for me, I live out back in the garden . . ." The little hand of the clock ticked to a minute before nine, and Sol shouted: "Excuse me, but I'll miss the bus . . ." And he broke into a run and collided in the swinging doors with the waiter, who made a whirling motion while carrying the whitecaps. Sol fell, and drenched in beer, he could not see, so he was on all fours in a puddle of beer, yelling and cursing. Vladimír was stunned, then recovered, stood up, buttoned up his coat, leaned over Sol, and quietly said: "Repeat over and over, 'stay calm, stay calm, stay calm.' If you should need something, my name is Vladimír, I work at the ČKD plant, just ask for me there, in a place called the boonies . . ." Another time Vladimír and I were sitting in Horkýs' in Libeň's Jewish quarter, each of us had bought ten bread rolls and was drinking Smíchov beer, the pub reverberating with conversation and laughter, workers scrubbed clean drinking coffee and rum by the window, when a man suddenly joined us and said: "Gentlemen, I am a married man, that in itself is not all that interesting, but, gentlemen, I live at my father-in-law's in a single room divided by a curtain. That my father-in-law eats my food, well, that's not particularly interesting, but, gentlemen, at night when I'm screwing my lawful wife on our side of the divide I can see at the head of my bed my father-in-law's silhouette on the curtain masturbating so adroitly that he comes at the moment I do. Gentlemen, where else in the world will you find such a father-in-law? My name isn't important, I'm just a simple housepainter." When Egon Bondy heard about the lashed out eyes, he dismissed it as banal with a wave of the hand, when he heard about Mr. Sol and Vladimir, he rubbed his hands in delight as our encounters with phenomenal events were already losing their intensity, no longer capable of being amplified, but when he heard about the father-in-law who masturbated by the head of his copulating daughter, he took me by the shoulder and squinted at me, he took my head in his hands and stared into my eyes to verify if this was the truth. And then he bellowed: "Where is this person?" I said: "Vladimír should be home soon." Bondy continued to yell: "The housepainter, where is he?" and he menacingly pointed his finger at my eyes: "Don't play with me, I know by now you want to put me off my writing, but you're fucking mistaken! You have to introduce me to the housepainter!" I said: "Right now he's painting the Cukrák tower, he's hanging by a rope and holding a brush in his hand, dipping it into the paint and singing away . . ." Bondy roared: "Bring me the painter!" And he covered his ears and squealed: "Vladimír has to write all of this down, and if he doesn't then you have to, like Božena Němcová did with fairy tales, and Jirásek with ancient legends. And tell Vladimír for me: The closer a mountain comes to the sun the colder it becomes . . . and only the sun is entitled to its spots, as Goethe said about Frederick the Great, King of Prussia, whom I'm studying at the moment. But you absolutely have to introduce me to this housepainter! Get it? I mean, he might be a martyr in the guise of a housepainter! This is what's at stake! The pope would say: 'The Church has no more need of martyrs!' We need them now more than ever, so bring me the painter! Fuck me Jesus . . . !"

One day I visited Vladimír when he was living on Kostnické Square, on the third floor. When his mother opened the door, I saw her tears glisten in the gloom of the foyer . . . I saw a door fly open and a stewpot fly through the air and tilt, the force of the heave dislodging gleaming cabbage with four or five dumplings, like beermats, all of which hovered in the light coming from the room, all of it flying over the illumined hallway and landing, per the laws of ballistics, at the door of Mrs. Boudníková, who was standing in the hall shouting: "It's marvelous you've come to visit us, Vlad will be so happy!" Then sotto voce: "What a night we've had, he's been carrying on like this!" And again loudly and resonantly: "You look great, Doctor, clearly you've been in the sun and swimming . . ." and quietly: "What a ruckus, the whole building could hear him . . ." and again loudly: "Please, do come in, Vlad has a new sweater. Vladimír! Oh . . . he'll be so happy!" And quietly: "He fell into a mirror and cut himself, and then he scrawled his blood over the wall and on a whole sheet of paper . . . it read: 'I shall become a priest of madness.'" I found Vladimír in a dejected state. He only said: "Mom's been on my back about me not showing appreciation for her putting food on the table, so I flung that little pot of hers." I said: "An unforgettable image, like something Salvador Dalí had photographed, things flying through the air and from the door someone pours out water and fish from an aquarium and cats in flight are going berserk from pouches tied to their tails . . ." Vladimír was ecstatic: "So you saw the pot fly through the air, and the cabbage . . . and the lighting, it was beautiful, wasn't it?" I said that it was and we should go to The Rosebush for a beer, that the publican and his wife each have a parakeet of their own and these parakeets swear at each other like sailors, and the two publicans just smile because without the parakeets doing it they'd be cursing each other . . . When I told Egon Bondy about the stewpot, he took fright then soon became delighted: "Fuck me Jesus! Nietzsche asked 'Where are the barbarians of the 20th century . . .' Vladimír, that's where! Of course! Vladimír! A barbarian of the twentieth age who swims in the frigid waters of art and in the warm waters of science, like Dalí said. Vladimír . . ."

One day as Vladimír and I were tramping around the Elbian countryside, a solitary tree came into view, offering all of itself to the sun, behind it dark woods. Again Vladimír was moved as he looked at it, smiling and nodding approvingly, in agreement with himself. "Look at this tree," he said, "it's Goethe, favorable conditions, branches outspread, taking in the Hellenistic sun on all sides, drinking from the earth what's needed to the point of satiety. But me, I'm a tree from those woods, my shoulders worn, reckoning only on the amount of sun able to reach my meager crown, all of us impinging on one another in these woods, encumbering one another, and yet we live our lives. I'm telling you," Vladimír continued, pointing to the solitary tree, "thanks to imagination and tactile experience I'm just as expansive as that Goethe over there. I have erased the difference between powerful individualism and the masses . . . Ha!" It was then that I began to understand that Vladimír's prints were the apotheosis of the fourth estate, the woods, the working class, that each encroaches on the other with their branches, that we're all condemned to live at the expense of the Universe and Beauty. And Vladimír continued to stand tenderly before that solitary tree and tenderly he said: "Just like this tree I also have all that is earthy in my leaves . . . To me this tree is vitreous, I see the sap extend as it climbs up the glass, I see it expand as it flows through the veins of the branches, I see blossoms, I see fruit . . . even the Earth is transparent for me, of glass, I'm able to follow the precise direction of roots and filaments, see them drink from the earth and water, I see the whole glass tree, each of its phases no matter the season of the year, and here and now I see the rings around which each part of the tree turns, I see the harmony of energy and sap . . . just a little imagination and everything becomes clear, and so much more human, don't you see, Doctor? Understand? Doctor . . . !" And at this moment I understood how Vladimír's prints were so wonderfully grounded, so connected to the earth, just like any good radio, any telephone, like those gasoline trucks trailing a chain sparking along the road as a ground to keep the gas from combusting during a thunderstorm. I saw that whenever Vladimír was feeling down he could always revive by bending down and touching a finger to the earth, and this gave him fresh energy and linked him to a mystical and yet very real communion. When Egon Bondy heard what Vladimír had said on our walk, he kicked the ribs of a radiator, and holding his ripped shoe hopped around the World Cafeteria and hollered: "That tree, this is old Jakob Böhme, that genius cobbler from Görlitz who removed the earth from trees to discover the relationship between matter and thought and to come up with the phrase: *Der als Mensch gewordene Gott!* Oyoyoy! I could kick my whole toe out of whack! But Vladimír! He's the fucking substrate of Hegel's entire philosophy, that tree! I'd have to study this a whole year, while that monster Vladimír blurts it out on a walk perfectly elucidated, as if he were just blowing his nose! Pure paranoia, I tell you! And I've completely ripped my shoe! You can be damn sure you're buying me a new fucking pair! . . ." Bondy raged, for him invective was a form of flattery . . . He later decided he would devote himself solely to art. And to get around the mandatory work law he decided to commit himself to the mental asylum. He enjoyed it well enough the first day and was wheedling Vladimír: "Look here, dear Vlado, this would be right up your alley, such a lovely institution, right near Prague, it's warm and cosy inside, food aplenty, they'll give you a pochade box and paper or canvas, you'll be allowed to go on walks and you can create in peace. And if you feel like going crazy, then you have paper to do it on, nothing will happen to you! . . ." But Vladimír had no thought of quitting the factory, which for him was more than an asylum, it was a refuge and a school and a lover, so he said no, no, and no. Egon Bondy showed up a month later, and whereas before he was pale, now he was tanned, weathered, but hopping mad, and right away he collapsed and started screaming: "Fuck me Jesus! To hell with the nuthouse! They've adopted Soviet methods that work is the best way to treat the somewhat maladjusted. So they gave me a hoe and every day I was out there weeding beetroot! I was feeling more and more healthy, but fuck me Jesus, rude health is nothing but a graveyard for poetry!" And having plopped down on the sofa he fell asleep, when he woke up three hours later he asked: "Doctor, you wouldn't by chance have any milk? And maybe some rye bread . . . ?"

Vladimír had decided to dive off the platform. He made the swimming trunks himself. Three days he worked on them, one side made of gauze and the other of black broadcloth. In reality the trunks consisted of two triangles connected by thin string, but it had to fit exactly right, so Vladimír stitched the swimsuit together and tried it on in front of the big mirror so he could get a view of the back, having purchased a small hand mirror for 4.60 crowns. I saw how he constantly held the small mirror at a distance so he could see in the big mirror how the trunks fit from the back. And it was quite the event when Vladimír, outfitted in this swimsuit of his, dove from the highest platform! He'd never dived before, just as he'd never played the violin or mandolin before and yet played them with feeling. Vladimír's verve was a marvel to behold as he started his run, both feet pattering on the surface, then he took flight with arms spread wide before slowly bringing them in toward his body as it turned down, and his two-meter frame sliced the water! Vladimír reemerged on the surface and after a few fathoms his hand smacked the edge of the pool, water dripping down his face as he dispensed advice to the lads: "Listen, the main thing is that when you jump keep your eyes on Vyšehrad in the distance, at first it seems to be sinking, but then as you turn down, keep glancing at it and you'll see Vyšehrad rapidly rising on the horizon at the same speed you're plummeting to the surface . . . Why am I telling you this? Always pay attention both to what you're doing and what's going on around you . . ." So Vladimír got out of the water and again solemnly, pedantically, ascended the steps to the highest diving platform, launched into his run-up, and his momentum compelled Vyšehrad to slightly curtsy and then swiftly rise up in his eyes, which shared with his body these legendary leaps of his from the diving tower's highest platform. When Egon Bondy heard about it he raved: "Fuck me Jesus! That Vladimír just keeps yanking my chain. Maybe now's a good time for me to dive head first into an empty swimming pool or from the tower of Saint Vitus. Well, Zbyněk Fišer's going to be blown away once I tell him this one!…"

Vladimír once borrowed a book from me that explained why the Hungarian national team was the best in the world then and why it had won the Match of the Century against England. He returned the book elated: "Doctor, what joy you've given me! That Hidegkuti juking on a dime, as they say, is a total game changer, his swerving in a tight space is just like my active prints on the same sort of confined surface!" When I told Egon Bondy about this, he was silent for a moment, and when the moment passed he was ten centimeters shorter. His weary voice quietly said: "That Vladimír, as I've said, he's a total paranoiac. About Hidegkuti's juking on a dime being akin to his active prints, no way I'm telling this to Zbyněk Fišer! He'd chide me for thinking it up myself…"

One time Vladimír fell for a chubby girl from Čimice. During a break at the Poldi steel mill he honored her by adjusting the power hammer exactly to the height of his nose and then lying down under it, and when one of his friends pressed the start button the hammer stopped exactly at his nose, just barely touching it. So one afternoon Vladimír had a date with his darling. As they were walking down the Čimice street at dusk, he honored her by removing his tie and securely fastening it around the branch of an apple tree and then quickly around his neck, nearly hanging himself, while the girl took off for home through the twilight. The next day, Vladimír returned with a photographer to the orchard in Čimice where his tie was still fastened to the branch, and he reenacted his declaration of love, his tongue lolling out a bit, and the photographer shot the whole thing. I was lounging at home in my bathrobe and slippers, and when Vladimír told me the story and showed me the photos, I wagged my head and flicked from my ears both the jolt of the power hammer and the hanging by necktie. Vladimír said: "So what should

I've done to please the girl, to give her some joy in life?" When I told Egon Bondy about it, he stuck his fingers in his ears and stamped his feet and yelled: "Enough, Doctor, for the love of God, enough! These stories about Vladimír are draining my life force, Doctor, I'll deflate like a leaky tire, so for mercy's sake, no more! Enough of this, I'm already riding on rims! That scumbag's punctured my soul! Fuck me Jesus! . . ."

Vladimír brought Kadel, a friend from work, home with him. Vladimír was always pulling his leg, not to rag on him but because he knew it would do him good. So they came home, Kadel in a panic. Vladimír said: "Kadel, did you notice that guy in a chauffeur's cap on our tail?" And Kadel would nod and look around dumbstruck, he was always wearing a cap with earflaps to keep from catching cold. And Vladimír: "If something happens, Kadel, where did you say you want to be buried, in Zbraslav or Modřany?" And Vladimír put a finger to his lips, tiptoed to the door, flung it open, and ran out into the evening courtyard. When he returned, Kadel's eyes were full of question marks. They took each other's hand, looked into each other's eyes, and vowed: "If something happens, then you, Kadel, heard and saw nothing!" The way home from work was full of mystery, whenever they showed up Kadel was always so filled with terror he was barely alive, only managing to remove his cap from his thinning hair and wipe away the sweat soaking his forehead. And the way he looked at Vladimír I saw that he couldn't live without him . . . well, he could, but with Vladimír there was mystery, during the day as well as at night, danger lurking everywhere . . . One time they were again holding hands in my room at 24 The Levee of Eternity, Vladimír ran outside to check if anyone was in the courtyard, and then he solemnly declared: "Starting today our password is: the Punkva to Dneprostroi." Then Vladimír sat down and while talking he reminded him en passant: "Listen, Kadel, make sure you bring long johns, it's cold in the joint, you know that, right?" Or: "Kadel, the back of your head's not hurting, is it? I don't want to scare you . . . but when the back of the head starts to hurt it's a sign of oncoming paralysis, you know that, right? Look, Kadel, have you made your Last Will yet? What do you think is the best way to go,

Kadel, being eaten by a shark or calcifying." And then he would again run out into the night.

One day Vladimír came home alone and all fired up. "Listen, Doctor, who would've thought it about Kadel? I can't keep inventing mysteries and passwords for him, so I wanted to teach him to make Explosionalist prints, and he got so angry at me that he straightened out this iron pair of compasses, must weigh a kilo, and chucked it at me, it brushed my hair as it whizzed past my ear before sticking into the cabinet and fluttering there a moment. Who would've thought? The guy almost has the same temperament as me, and he made me really happy with that compass." When Egon Bondy heard about this, he murmured while giving me the side-eye: "I can't even get upset about this anymore. So, the Punkva to Dneprostroi? That Vladimír is master of the world . . . or what . . . good thing I've written *Prague Life*, that I've composed *The Large Book* and *The Small Book* and other poetry collections . . . but what should I do? Little by little pack away the writing implements, quietly lock the typewriter in the cabinet, and then culti-vate Indian philosophy with Zbyněk Fišer, who will teach me Sanskrit, the train will enter the tunnel so that in a couple of years I can bud again like a mystically germinating plant . . . So the Punkva to Dneprostroi, huh? For pity's sake, Doctor, that Vladimír is such a torment for me! Ugh! Fuck me Jesus! . . ."

The director of Crooked Wheel Gallery saw Vladimír's prints at the home of the poet Jiří Kolář and decided on the spot to organize an exhibition for him in Warsaw. He rolled up the prints sans official stamps, undid his pants and shirt, and placed them on his belly, then buttoned up his fly and shirt, and this is how Vladimír flew from Prague to the Crooked Wheel in Warsaw. And because there was no paper for a catalogue, the poet Kolář discovered that letters up to 4.5 kg could be sent by airmail to Warsaw, so he cut up wrapping paper into parcels each weighing 4.5 kg, and from all the post offices in the Prague suburbs letters weigh-ing 4.5 kg were mailed to Warsaw, Crooked Wheel, Attn.: Mr. Marian Bogusz, who then had catalogues printed on the paper. And Director Davis of the Institute of Modern Art in Miami saw the prints at the Crooked Wheel exhibition, so

Vladimír's artwork flew across the ocean and had a celebrated exhibition there. From that time on Vladimír was afraid to get a haircut. As soon as he saw the scissors in the hands of the barber he went numb with fear, what if the barber was making prints in the evenings and was jealous of him, and then out the blue jabbed the open scissors into his eyes all the way into his brain? So his mother cut his hair, and later this task fell to his beloved wife, Tekla. This was always an event, these haircuts, so much fuss, so much looking in the mirror before Vladimír decided that his hair was cut exactly as if it had never been cut, since he was incorrigibly enamored with having foppishly disheveled hair and Baudelaire's or Brummell's studious disregard for their dress. But when Tekla was cutting up and shredding clothing to sell the fabric as scrap, she constantly brandished the scissors at Vladimír's eyes. So every time she cut his hair he always thought he would end up blind, because Tekla would gesticulate with the scissors while giving him the haircut and chastise him for not bringing home more money, that they had a total of two crowns fifty in cash. When Egon Bondy heard about this, his chin drooped and his legendary, magnificently red lips glistened like cherry pulp, his blue eyes shifted in grief, and he said: "Everyone knows that no permission is required for air to stream and water to flow across state borders, that birds fly through the sky wherever they need to without a passport, but for pity's sake, how am I to accept that Vladimír flies in a crotch across state borders without permission as if God? All in all I suppose that might be okay, but fuck me Jesus! why do I have to know about those spectacular episodes with the scissors? What have I done to anyone that no woman has ever wanted to gouge out my eyes from love?"

Vladimír liked pubs that were heated either with coal or wood in a Musgraves 14 stove or in one of those giant black Filaks, the kind that resembled a fireproof strongbox. So we sat by the window at Horkýs', snow falling outside, and Vladimír melancholically gazed into the taproom where the barman, Mr. Šoler, was stoking the stove before continuing with his whistling and pouring his legendary Smíchov 10° lager. Snow had been falling since morning, groups of boys burst into the scene, two sides pelting each other with snowballs. One group was eventually overwhelmed by the other and fell back. "That stove in the corner, it's me, when you don't feed it, it doesn't give off heat . . . watch this," Vladimír said while observing the boys throwing snowballs, and he ran out just as he was, into the snowstorm, he kneeled down, then leaned on his elbows in the snow, and then was on all fours, his back like a bench. It's happened, I said to myself, he's completely lost his mind, like Egon Bondy said, pure paranoia, classic schizo. Yet Vladimír was grinning, he twisted his head to the window, the customers looked, one felt sorry for him, another was shocked, yet Vladimír was grinning and displaying that sagacious smile he always had when confronted with a mystery about to be revealed. And I also began to grin because as the boys tossing snowballs began to back up, one of them was coming dangerously close to Vladimír, who was patiently waiting, like astronomers for a solar eclipse they have calculated to the day and second. And Vladimír, stationary, on all fours in the snow, waited for his eclipse, the boy, who had just tossed a snowball, fell over Vladimír's back, tumbling backward magnificently like a footballer executing a scissors kick over his head, and startled by the unexpected obstacle he just lay there. Vladimír extended his hand and lifted the boy to his feet and then took some snow in his hand and packed it into a lovely ball, the boy joined in and the tables turned and in no time the boys couldn't withstand the superior force and took off around the corner of Václav Šimůnek's sweetshop, formerly a purveyor of suet, as the inscription on the building's façade reads to this day.

One time Vladimír left for a weeklong volunteer work brigade. He returned stoked, sanctified, but with a limp. He explained: "It was glorious, Doctor! The whole day my hands in the dirt, digging potatoes, I have the entire globe within me, Mother Earth, soil. But! What a treat! I was tying my shoes and all of a sudden oof, I was flying ten meters though the air in an arc, and when I landed I turned around and it was an irate ram, you know, nearly all males are jealous of me. The shepherd, Němec, comes running up and says, 'He does that a lot,' and then continues on his way with his flock of sheep. Well, it was amazing! But I passed out only once. In the evening I was washing my feet in a vat and sitting on a bench and out of the blue a cowherd is driving his cows past . . . One of the cows looks over at me and breaks into a run straight for me, just like women throw themselves at me. I look up and the cow is already breathing on me, drooling on my knees, but she does a snowplow, bends down, and drinks up all the water in one go and then sucks my toes to boot. The cowherd runs up to calm me down: 'There's not much water around here . . . she does this a lot.' And I fainted, no one had ever sucked my toes before. I tell you, Doctor, next time I have a chance I'm volunteering for that work brigade again." Later, when Vladimír got married for a second time, he took his bride for their honeymoon to a farm, also a work brigade, to dig potatoes. He returned disappointed . . . "Doctor, fortune no longer smiles on me, no ram, no thirsty cow, only bad luck now, no incidents, I tell you, fortune has turned its back on me, maybe forever." When Egon Bondy heard about the jealous ram and the thirsty cow, right on the street he started to gently bang his head against a wall and beat the plaster with both fists while shouting: "Fuck me Jesus! This is Saint Francis through and through! That Vladimír is always in a state of grace and it will never ever stop favoring him! Fuck me Jesus, looks like another night with sleep in the crapper!"

Vladimír always experienced things as if it were for the first time, like a stranger, like a child. When we went to a football match, first he would stare in amazement, then he would launch into a series of questions, which uniform is Slavia's, which the opponent's, then: what is offside, what is a goal, what is out, what is a foul. When the spectators had screamed and shouted their fill at Vladimír, he would then finally declare that such a match is the exact image of what happens in a magnetic field, and when the match was even, he was overjoyed that it was the image of a true print, two opposites in a state of equilibrium that it was possible to trace the field lines formed by the movement of the attack and the defense, and what really delighted him was when the play of the ball had both teams in motion. But to him the most beautiful thing about football was when the players streamed and flowed into a vacuum as the movement of one or the other team attempted to achieve a numerical advantage over their opponent. He ultimately arrived at the insight that the game of football resembles the door of a pub withstanding the impact of ten people trying to get out while ten people are simultaneously trying to get in. One time we were at the Slavoj VIII football club for a tournament of deaf-mute teams. The match became even more of a ballet full of movement and gesticulation when a foul was called as the players gesturally pleaded to the referee how wrong they felt the call was, all of it a wondrous silent film, a pantomime, a dance interlude. That whole night and a long time thereafter Vladimír held forth on the relationship between football and Explosionalist printmaking, and in the evening at the King Wenceslas, where the ladies came freshly coiffed and all decked out in their very best, and former footballers from Meteor and SK Libeň and Čechie Karlín came by, and all waited for the dark-haired footballer who lived in Libeň's Jewish quarter to show up, straddle a chair, and recount all the football matches, everyone waiting solely for this former Adonis and his commentary. When Vladimír reported on the one match he had seen over the past three months, everyone present was transfixed by his magnificent portraits of the players and stupendous observations of the important moments in the match . . . and when he finished, a fortifying cordial was distributed to the ladies and a large cognac brought to Vladimír for such a gripping account, and the former players winked at one another, as they considered Vladimír off his rocker, his descriptions of football so spellbinding and from an angle completely different than how the game is usually viewed . . .

For Vladimír, the sanatorium was a world of normality, a world of striving citizens desiring consumer products represented as an arithmetic mean. When he was a miserable wreck on the verge of madness, he embraced the game of this world so he could relax, recharge his battery. He would lower the wick of his overheated lamp to keep the glass cylinder from bursting and go out shopping or to the cinema, and later he even took up fishing. In these moments he was a completely different person, and even if he observed consumer society from the heights of a satellite, sometimes he liked to play a participant in it, like children gleefully visiting a funhouse, hall of mirrors, planetarium, or Julius Fučík Amusement Park. It could be said that ordinary folk pushed him higher, their obtuse egomania driving him to be someone else, to dress like them, to walk to work as they did, to scorn all those *Allzumenschliches*, the "all too human," and extend his imagination by scaling a ladder, climbing up to the last rung into the beautiful storm clouds . . .

When Vladimír was planning to marry Tekla, they first asked my advice if I thought it would be better for her to study art aesthetics or languages or go to graphic design school. She ultimately ended up working at the same place where Vladimír had apprenticed on the lathe, and she wore bib overalls, thanks to which her lovely breast became the darling of the factory. After his shift, Vladimír would sit in the women's locker room under the clock and start up a conversation with the showering female workers about conjugal life in such detail that the women blushed to the very roots of their hair. Vladimír deplored the fact that Tekla had to bathe at the factory. When she didn't go to work he bathed her himself in a washtub. So she would have some good things in life, he liked to parade before her in the nude with an impressive erection. When the female coworkers became concerned that Vladimír might find this exhausting, he reassured them that he does this and other things as well for his wife to bring some joy and experiences to her life. Most of all Vladimír preferred to sit with a lesbian worker who liked to shower with Tekla. Admiring his wife's body, he and the lesbian would quietly chat, and these enamored two shared their experiences and impressions, always finding agreement, even though they were of opposite sexes. They whispered so loudly the other workers blushed even more and looked at Vladimír with admiration and wished that each woman had a husband at home as loving as him. When Egon Bondy heard about this, he squealed: "You're doing this again on purpose, that lesbian was whispering with Vladimír on purpose to keep me from hearing about anything they said! That Vladimír! Fuck me Jesus! I, who thought I was a specialist in these matters because I adhere to the ancient Gnostic teaching that spiritual life is achieved only through sexual perversion. So, that Vladimír is ridiculing me in the factory, is he? That Vladimír is relentless, absolutely relentless!" I whispered to Egon: "If I remember correctly, one time on The Levee of Eternity Vladimír stuck a Christmas tree candle all the way up his nose . . ." Bondy thundered: "For fuck's sake, a Christmas tree candle, up his nose? . . ." I said: "Up his nose . . ." Egon Bondy scampered around, kicked his feet in the air, and then held his knees: "Now my calf's cramping, but why the fuck up his nose?" I said: " Because he wanted the tactile experience of homosexuality . . . I had to pull it out with pliers and good thing the wick was still visible . . ." And Egon Bondy threw me to the ground and wriggled his chin across my face and hollered: "When you two aren't looking I'll kill you, kill you both, just kill you . . ." He then pushed me away, and looking up at the firmament called out in ecstasy: "Paris is right here in Prague, in Libeň. And altogether it is Galicia. The son of the Rabbi of Belz is Vladimír. Like I said, paranoia pure and simple . . . !"

One day Egon Bondy wanted to visit Vladimír and Tekla a couple of weeks after their wedding. I said: "We need to go to Na Žertvách because they've got a basement flat in the building where Jiří Šmejkal lives, he just had the space white-washed." It was evening when we arrived at their door. The shutters were closed, but not tightly, so through a five-centimeter slit Vladimír could be seen walking back and forth in the neon light, his curly fair hair continuously ablaze, spectacu-lar, Vladimír's bust, as if flickering within reach waist-deep in a grave, yet he was speaking as he darted around the long basement. And then Tekla came into view, an attractive young lady resembling a damsel of noble blood, running behind Vladimír and telling him something, but Vladimír was all worked up, agitated, exasperated to the point of lunacy, the freshly whitewashed walls gleaming. So Vladimír and Tekla flitted around, their hands gesticulating, Vladimír scolding Tekla about something and she defending herself, the basement charged like a Leyden jar. Egon Bondy panted and wheezed as he squatted: "Fucking hell, that Vladimír is a real piece of work. It's going to end in catastrophe!" And he was right. Stupendous in his anger and rebukes, Vladimír raved and hurled lightning from his hand at Tekla, who several times dropped to her knees before him, but Vladimír violently shook free of her grip and dragged her behind his long legs. I turned around, and across the tracks, on the other side of Na Žertvách Street with its single-story houses, light came from an open window on the first floor, under the bulb in this window the partially painted portrait of a nude woman reclining on a settee, the artist working on it with his back to the window, and every time he removed his gaze from the room's corner, where the other window was closed and festooned with green blinds, he would apply the color of his expressionist emotion elicited by the female flesh, his prodigious passion plastering and flinging it onto the canvas with a brush. I said, "Bondy, look . . . ," and gripped his shoulder, but at that moment a locomotive was chugging down Na Žertvách in white steam, majestically thick smoke covering the building across the street as well as us. When it had passed and the smoke cleared, Bondy trained his eyes on the open window and the painter's back, on his head turning back and forth, and then on the earnest work on the portrait of the woman lying in the quiet of the room with her legs spread. Egon Bondy placed a bemused finger on his red lip, then turned around and looked through the chink at Vladimír, who at the height of his exasperation had produced a bucket with tar and dipped a brush into it and started to lay down with powerful motions black stripes on the white wall, flicking tar splatters onto the wall, completely giving himself over to the rhythm of his Explosionalist mania, eventually calming down, though he now disappeared with his work from the slit in the shutters, the sound of the brush intermittently scraping against the bucket reverberating . . . and through the chink Tekla came into view, she stood there watching Vladimír work, rancor and fear fell from her to the same general degree her face and hands and bearing ricocheted information to us about what was hap-pening out of sight . . . Egon was waiting by the other basement window for Vladimír to appear in the chink between shutter slats, which was wider, so we ran back and forth from one window to the other, from Tekla, who now was actually speaking, her hand exhorting Vladimír and giving him strength and courage . . . and so I was the one who saw his long shadow and maniacal work trashing Jiří's basement. Vladimír's shadow drew closer and passed as first his hand appeared and then he did in his entirety. Egon Bondy whispered: "Doctor, what we're wit-nessing is genuine obscenity, the revelation of a secret, this is brilliant, I'm going to consult Zbyněk Fišer about this . . ." An electric current surged through Vladimír's whole body and he flew three meters, now he reappeared excited, focused, his face brightened, serene, radiating joy at the climax that was slowly approaching, the splotches and splatters discharged from the fierce rhythm of the brush dipped in the bucket of tar were all agleam, and just as he'd always dreamed about putting a tarred loo through the etching press, he now worked to create a tarred wall to ventilate a suffering whose import we could not know. And no sooner had we turned around than we saw that the painter's back was now erect and had stepped back, and the portrait of the mass of radiant female flesh was adorned with hair on the crotch and underarms and on a head ablaze in polychrome, and as the painter's energy had waned in direct proportion to the painting's power, he slumped into a chair, his hands hanging limp across his knees like two towels, and a woman's hand took the porcelain knob and pulled it and with a loud clatter the blinds surged and were sucked upward . . . While Vladimír, having defaced all the walls of this giant cellar, slowly came in, as if his footsteps were stuck in the thickening tar, taking awhile to go from the second chink in the shutters to the first . . . he was about ten centimeters shorter, stooped, the wrinkles around his mouth drooping like two mustaches . . . Tekla slowly walked behind him lost in thought, then they went across the hallway into the other room, which they called the "office," the cellar went dark. Egon Bondy turned around and the light also went out on the first floor. Bondy was silent, he held out his hand, extending his delicate girl's hand to show me how his fingers were trembling, just nodding his head, hair falling over his forehead, looking like Dionysus with a hangover . . .

The next day Tekla rushed over and was wringing her hands while standing in the courtyard as she cried out: "Doctor, Doctor, for God's sake, Doctor! Quick, come to our place, Vladimír's gone crazy!" I grabbed my coat and on the way I tried to find out what the problem was, but Tekla just wrung her hands. When I went into the cellar, the shutters were still closed, the odor of broken fluorescent bulbs pervaded the chilly cellar air while outside the sun was shining. Vladimír lay in bed by the wall, and the wall was glittering with tar blotches and splatters, the whole cellar resembled a stilt house with black trunks everywhere around it, a fence of dark planks punctured by the mighty impact of grapeshot and projectiles discharged from a brush dipped in asphalt. And Vladimír's entire head was bedecked with dark welts and bumps growing menacingly, some sticking up like horns. I said: "My God, Vladimír, what on earth happened to you?" To show rather than speak, he lifted himself up and repeatedly butted his head against the wall, relishing the concussive jolts to his brain from hammering his head, his forehead imprinted with tar and whitewash from the wall. I leapt on him and pulled him down, but he wrenched free with a monstrous maniacal force. Tekla jumped on him, but he broke free of both of us as if we were children, and again started to beat his head against the wall, and again we pulled him away and out of the bed to the middle of the cellar, but he dragged the both of us toward the wall as if we weighed no more than our clothes and started to bash his head against it, the powerful blows vibrating through our hands . . . until he nearly passed out from the last blow and collapsed and let us carry him to the bed. I placed my hand on his brow and felt his head swell up as contusions and welts formed. Tekla soaked towels that we placed on his forehead one after the other, the route from the hallway faucet glittering with drops of water as she brought the compresses . . . I then suggested she go out to get some Burow's solution and plenty of cotton balls and gauze . . . Rushing up the stairs, her right shoe landing on the street, I saw her legs run past the shutters through a chink . . . Vladimír was rallying . . . I said: "Vladimír, what were you freaking out about this time, what made you hurt yourself like this, what's going on with you?" Vladimír turned his head to the side of the pillow and bathed in tears murmured: "She told me about those guys who had their way with her, and when they'd finished how they left her lying in the meadow and eating the rippled dirt of a molehill in her misery . . . it really got to me . . . I wanted to help her . . . I wanted to take that malice, what happened to her, onto myself to diminish it . . . And I also wanted her to know that I would do anything for her . . . to bring her joy, some experiences, that I belong to that heroic generation that takes life seriously . . . understand?" It was silent for a moment, feet walking up and down the sidewalk, some quickly, some leisurely, as if each person were carrying their destiny by Vladimír's cellar. . . Then the door flew open, first I saw Tekla gingerly run through, her hands full of gauze and packages of cotton wool . . . I saw how she quickly got her bearings before the closed door, like a rat, then lifted her leg and used the sole of her shoe like a hand to push the door handle, and upon entering bump the door with her butt to close it. We proceeded to bandage Vladimír, first sprinkling on antiseptic powder and dousing the cotton wool with Burow's solution. Then I stood on the last step and had to lean forward to see the bed. Tekla was sitting at its head, and because she didn't know what else to do she fluffed up the pillow and straightened out the corners behind Vladimír's head, whose beatific eyes were turned upward toward her fingers . . . "Okay?" I asked. "Okay," Tekla replied, and Vladimír smiled and softly exulted: "Hahahaha . . ."

I saw two people with the thumbprint of God on their brows: Vladimír and Egon Bondy. Two ornaments of materialistic thought, two Christs in the guise of Lenins, two romantics to whom it had been granted at the age of twenty-five the ability to plumb the retinal field of the university library . . .

Vladimír and I were fond of the World Cafeteria because Mrs. Vlaštovková was always in a good mood and the beer was even better. But when we learned the history of the World Palace with its cafeteria and sit-down restaurant and cinema, we attended every event. There used to be an estate in what was once the Jewish quarter whose owner was named Svět, or World. He mulled over his name and considered it no coincidence that it meant World. So he sold the whole estate and borrowed money on top of that and had the World Palace built. The cinema opened with a showing of the American epic film *Deluge*, but what about the groundwater from the Vltava! While it was raining on the screen, and it was pouring down, and Noah's Ark was sailing through the torrential downpour, in the cinema's basement groundwater from the Vltava was seeping through, the spectators up to their knees in water, but the film must continue to the end. So landowner Svět lost a million crowns on the cinema. He shot himself. Now you can hear the pumps working during each showing. Above the restaurant is a green globe with the letters SVĚT. When Vladimír took Egon Bondy to the World Cinema and he heard the pumps and about the history, he screamed during the newsreel: *"Yebem ti boga tryskovego!* Three-hundred cinemas in Prague and only a single one near Vladimír! Fuck me Jesus! Ugh, ugh, and ugh!"* He was spluttering and carrying on and right when the newsreel was showing the reception of a states-man from a friendly country, the ushers switched on the lights and led Bondy away while reminding him that his shouting could have unforeseen consequences for the entire world . . .

We were sitting one morning drinking Pilsner at The Slavic Linden, first on the restaurant's back patio, then, following the sun, in the courtyard. We looked up at the gallery with a St. John of Nepomuk large as a man. The guys at our table were talking filth: "She had one like this, you know, a butcher's dog would be all up in that thing, you could put it around its neck like a collar. I tell you, sexual intercourse with a wife after five years of marriage should be declared incest and punished with time in the slammer. Hers was like a yawning ox." We took our pints and repaired to the taproom. A young lad with freshly bandaged eyes joined us at the table, and when he drank he had to cock back his head as if he were gargling. "It's nothing," he began to say, but after he'd downed two beers he said, "I got arc eye. I'm a welder." And then he went on at length about a girl. Summer night. Hand on her panties. But his rubber broke. He didn't go any further. "She was a beauty, but the broken rubber made me go limp. When this stuff happens to me," he added, "I slap myself silly." This inspired Vladimír to think of Tekla, and he said: "My short-comings are my strength. Sometimes I have such a buildup of pressure in my head that I could use a bleeding valve. What can I do? She bailed on me . . . I'm wearing her panties. The second pair. The first got ripped. I put them in a wrapper. Look, I have her sweater on. It's more loose threads now than a sweater. She wanted to have money, so she left, while I'm falling to pieces . . . The girl who inspired louts didn't even give me that. I'd really like to have some sign from her, I'd write her letters with my dick . . . ," Vladimír exclaimed before running out to the patio, then he stood in the courtyard leaning against a wall in the sun, tears streaming down his face, and he didn't wipe them away. I paid, and we walked down the lively avenue, passersby thinking that Vladimír's mother or child had just died, we were crossing on red, but the traffic cop swung his striped baton for us to continue, indicating that he understood, even stopping cars, so we crossed as if we were an ambulance, a motorcycle cop speeding to a fire or a car pileup. We ended up at the King George in Libeň. Once we got there Vladimír wiped his tears and we took a seat at a table where a drunken carpenter from Kotlaska Street sat passed out. Then a young man showed up sporting a massive bald spot that actually looked good on him. He set a small sack of fledgling pigeons on the table. The squabs were trying to stand and kept falling. The young guy smacked his hand on the table and the pigeons went silent, likely toppling over. Someone at a neighboring table was bringing a conversation to a close: "And so, gentlemen, Hašek was a force of nature, by the age of forty he'd written one novel and 600 stories, who can top that? Well?" And the drunken carpenter raised his head and said: "I've made 600 armoires in my life. And this Hašek? This dirtbag? My wife read him and got such a wild hair she skipped out on me. Hašek ruined my marriage," the drunkard said, and before he could put his head back down he spread his elbows apart on the tablecloth and, to give emphasis to his words, his fists whacked the sack where the little pigeons where still trying to stand on their feet. The sack sagged and blood seeped out forming an ever-expanding stain on the white tablecloth. The handsome bald man sighed in relief: "Well, at least I don't have to choke them . . ." Vladimír jumped up, his face radiant: "Doctor, I'm a wimp! Will you buy me ten quartos of paper? And inks? How much will I need? OK, let's go . . ." He pointed at the stain from the flattened pigeons and at the drunk and shouted in the doorway: "Reality has a head start on me . . . tonight I'll try to catch up to it . . ."

Vladimír's entire life resembled the work of a human heart that thinks. He picked out and selected only those experiences that were compatible with his type, that is to say, not every experience, only those that simultaneously possessed a creative sensibility and thought. His criterion was always the presence of a trembling and pealing in the whole of his being, a signal system that had been with him since childhood, since the very beginning of his life, plasma, sperm flowing along all umbilical cords back to the smooth seamless belly of the Ur-mother, Eve. So Vladimír's art is a *regressus ad originem*, letting haptic sensation swallow him up in the maternal womb, pulling over his head one vagina after another as if a sweater, returning to the Great Mother like Goethe once did. Yet Vladimír's return, his *regressus od originem*, is simultaneously a *progressus ad futurum*. The circle closes, the first day of the world's creation linked to its end . . . eternity . . .

Erection and ejaculation had a transcendental nature for Vladimír, his sperm capable of impregnating a virgin, the spurting of fuel to directly under the spark plug without the mediation of a carburetor. The resistance of the material the only question . . . and the work of thought! Grace! Even the Catholic God is able to act directly, without causal nexus, without a carburetor. Ignite! And that's how it is, solid as a Helvetic Confession. Anna Hea Mulge. Father, Son, and Holy Spirit. The Immaculate Conception of the Virgin Mary, deflowered absent a carburetor, directly by the power of Spirit alone. So it was with Vladimír. Anointed in his own semen is how he worked, and anointed thus he smeared the etching press when he executed a take down and applied a Finnish armlock and then a double Nelson to it, his jism daubing everything, even the infant the press's vagina discharged on the other side in the form of a print. Lightning is the shortest way to the earth and into the earth . . .

So what culminated in an extreme subject ultimately culminated in objectification and became an independent world that acted on Vladimír, instantaneously affecting him, a direct line intermittently calling him through the movement of matter within matter, his printmaking propelling him straight into a space where human thought does not yield. Through relative freedom he attained an absolute lack of freedom requiring no explication, no justification, in which a man is what he is. Identity of the music of the spheres and the things strewn over this earth. Absolute game, *fruitio Dei*, monad of monads, *ens realissmum, Ding an sich selbst*, a cave not with the shadow of things but where the very ideas themselves are beheld. So in this way he penetrated and surpassed those places beyond us. Vladimír, as the firstborn Son of God, invoked matter and action to reinstate drama as an active love for the Universe and Humankind.

I often had to tell Vladimír two stories, which for some unknown reason had a profound effect on him. One was the story of Sep Bruml and his friend, who so liked to swap anecdotes that they would walk together back and forth several times across Libeň Bridge. Sep accompanied his friend in the elevator up to his apartment, but since their dialogue was far from finished they took the elevator back down and crossed the bridge to take the elevator up to Sep's apartment, who already had the key in the door, but since the conversation was not yet over, they took the elevator back down and Sep accompanied his friend back to Libeň … But what Vladimír considered the most beautiful tale was the one about the friendship between Headmaster Kocourek from Velenka and Headmaster Talacek from Semice, who when they had finished drinking beer in the pub accompanied one another, crowned with stars, through the tunnel of night, and always when one or the other was at his door, they found that one owed the other a walk to his place, and besides, the problem of educating the young needed so much more fleshing out that they would walk another three kilometers to the other's home. And so they kept each other company like this until dawn during the summer months, and only fatigue was able to send these two headmaster chums to bed. When Headmaster Talacek went to Prague from Poříčany, the friends would agree on the train he would return on, and then Headmaster Kocourek would leave the pub at exactly the right time so they could meet up halfway in Chrást, in Mandršejd, or Manso, so they could discuss what was new, and there was always so much new to talk about that when they arrived at Semice the headmaster put his briefcase away and the friends then walked together to Velenka. Whenever Vladimír heard this he melted, his unblinking eyes followed the routes of the two headmasters, and he came to the conclusion that the two men must be very happy. And when I told Vladimír that just recently I learned that the daughter of Headmaster Kocourek had fallen in love with a handsome fellow from Manso, but the headmaster didn't approve of their union, so the lad went to the forest and shot himself in the head and the girl placed her hanky under his bleeding head and then she leaped into the Elbe at Přívlaky, when Vladimír heard this, he gazed into the very heart of this doomed loved and said: "I would really like to have such a friendship. And did these two friends continue their walks?" I told him what I heard, that they did, even though both were retired, so they had more opportunities to shuttle between the door in Velenka and the door in Semice and back again, and when they couldn't, they wrote each other every day, sending messages and news. Later Vladimír and I no longer spoke about these events, maybe we even forgot about them, yet when we had something to talk about, Vladimír would accompany me to Libeň only for us to walk back again, from The Levee of Eternity to be standing again on Kostnické Square before the door of his building, into which he had already inserted the key, but then, having thought about it, pulled it back out and walked with me through Pražačka to The Levee of Eternity, while headmasters Talacek and Kocourek hovered above us like the clouds of an idealized superstructure in a Baroque painting. During the time when Vladimír moved out from his mother's place to a garret in Old Town and from there to my place in Libeň, only to return to his mother, entangled in an umbilical cord not by an Oedipal complex but a Mother complex as a symbol of creation, during this time when we went on walks together, we conjectured that as two sons born to single mothers we didn't suffer from an Oedipal complex, and what a wonderful calling it was to despise the father and live only for oneself, only through a Son complex and have no other model other than oneself alone, while never becoming a model oneself, and if so, then a model whose essence is disdain for all models, so to live at the expense of oneself and the Universe, to engage in a never-ending war with oneself alone, to make peace, which will never be made, to always be in a state of creative tension and intoxication. When Egon Bondy heard about these conversations, he shouted: "I won't get angry at Vladimír anymore. I'll just kill him and that'll be the end of it! I mean, everything he says is exactly how I live my life, as a Marxist lefty in a state of permanent revolution, in a state of perpetual revolt against the Father because up till now the Son has taken the place of every Father killed, so becoming the Father who has to wait until someone kills him . . . but fuck me Jesus, we are only sons forever . . . long live permanent revolution . . . !"

I was best man at Vladimír's first wedding. When the bridal procession was about to get underway I said: "For Christ's sake, Vladimír, you forgot the tie!" So he quickly put on a regular necktie since he couldn't find the white wedding one. When we came to the town hall and the procession was forming, the lady official whispered something to Vladimír, and voila, he had two ties. As excited as he'd been in the morning, the tie had shifted all the way over to his collarbone, so he ended up having two. Otherwise he rarely wore a tie, and in summer he wore it only at half mast and with such incomparable panache it was if he'd spent the entire night writing poetry and partying. Still drowsy one morning in Libeň, we got a real fright when Vladimír's foot swelled up so much he couldn't get his shoe on, so he put on a slipper and that afternoon we went to the polyclinic straight to Dr. Adam. Through the door we heard his benevolent, calming voice: "Come now, mother, don't cry, lass, take off your clothes, I won't bite, come now, lass, you can't be afraid of me when I'm about as old as you, come now . . ." And when we entered the white doctor's office, Vladimír leaning on me, Dr. Adam with his pince-nez and shaved head, looking peerlessly human, said: "So what's the problem, you two imbeciles, you got soused, eh? Show me, moron . . ." And Vladimír pulled out his foot, and the doctor examined the painfully swollen foot . . . And then he opened the door and kindly shouted to the full waiting room: "Scram, you two idiots, before I kick you in the ass down the stairs all the way to Palmovka and under a tram . . ." And we ran out as Dr. Adam explained to the waiting room and our backs receding in the distance: "That cretin was so sloshed he put three socks on the same foot!" When he heard about Vladimír's swollen foot, Egon Bondy called out to the heavens: "I can't be friends with Vladimír anymore, but before I end it I'll get him to join the Club of Prague Pranksters, headed by the son of the owner of Schönbach Funeral Home . . . ! That Vladimír is greater than any Dadaist, or Hašek, similar to me in a way. Fuck me Jesus, this whole business will make mince-meat of me . . . !"

We sat on the curb with three other drinkers on Bratrská Street. It was half past noon and we had beermats on the curb for the pints we were slowly drinking. Behind us the pub, Přemysl's, an establishment that used to house the carters and coachmen syndicate, had its shutters lowered, when Egon Bondy came marching down Na Žertvach, his steps becoming unsteady once he spotted us from afar. Vladimír offered him a spot next to him, first spreading out a handkerchief because Bondy was wearing new pants, so-called leisure slacks. "So what the fuck are you doing out here?" Bondy asked, taking a sip of beer, the extra one we'd brought to the curb. Vladimír whispered: "The publican, when it comes over him, so around twice a week, he shoos us out, locks up, and says: 'Why should I torture myself . . . ?'" "What the hell?" said Bondy, horrified. "He really really likes his wife," whispered Vladimír, "so when the mood strikes, you know, the customers have to wait outside for half an hour." "Holy shit, fuck me Jesus, how young is the guy?" Bondy said alarmed. And suddenly the shutters rumbled behind us and were wholly sucked up to the ceiling in a rollicking clatter. Old man Bureš in a white apron came out, the customers got up, each with their beermat and now empty glass, and went back into the pub, each to his place from before. Egon Bondy looked in turn at old man Bureš, at his wife, her hair streaked with gray but her face flushed, he looked at her pouring beer, as if nothing . . . And Bondy quietly exclaimed: "You're putting me on. Vladimír! Doctor! You've put them up to this to crush me! I've worked a whole week on Zen Buddhism only for you, on the fact that Russia is Gogol rather than Dostoevsky, and you spring this *happening* on me, it's going to take a lot for me to recover from it. Fuck me Jesus . . . !"

Vladimír and I would often frequent a booze joint called The Hamlet, and not because we liked the rye in those square shot glasses, but because it was a dive without windows, so Vladimír liked to stand in the gloom, particularly when it was a lovely sunny day out, and as light only came in through the glass panel door, he had the sensation of wearing his black hat pulled down over his brow and striding down the street. Later we would go to The Hamlet fifteen minutes before the proprietor opened up, removing the iron bar and throwing open the heavy oak doors in the form of two angel wings. During those fifteen minutes prior to the joint's opening, an elderly lady would show up holding a tin cup and take a seat on the steps and wait, five minutes before opening she'd get antsy and go to the door, put her ear to it, and listen in terror lest the barkeep had died or something. When she heard life coming from inside, she gently tapped her tin cup on the iron bolt, as if she were buried in a collapsed mine and giving a sign to rescuers. When the doors opened, she was the first to dart inside, buying two deciliters of rye and immediately downing it while standing, tears of joy running down her face, and then she would order another for her cup and sit on the steps and sip it, and after that she took her cup home, spry and bright, filled with joy. Vladimír inquired: "Tell me, if you don't mind, how old is that lady?" The barkeep rinsed the glasses and poured us another deci of rye against the light and said: "Seventy-six, she'll be back in the evening." Vladimír said: "Doctor, let's drink to the lady's health. When she's ninety she'll find a world-famous doctor and live to a hundred and thirty, folks like her have immortal lungs." "Got that right," said the barkeep, pouring a rye, and he added: "When I see that granny drink with such gusto from her tin cup I get a hankering for a little nip too!" And he raised a square shot glass, which glittered like a Venetian glass chandelier, clicked his heels, and knocked back the shot. Vladimír and I poured out a little of the rye in our hands and rubbed it on our faces and in our hair and then carefully rubbed some on the napes of our necks. "It's good for slipped discs," Vladimír said, and smelling of anise we went out into the sun to walk three buildings down for a beer at Ferkl's, to stretch our legs . . .

Vladimír and I would got to Hausmans' in slippers since it was right around the corner. I had brought a bicycle to Prague from Nymburk, and one time I borrowed a second one, we put an alarm clock in the satchel, one of those awful Rosskopf double bells that could wake people several streets away when it went off, and we took a little trip to Hausmans'. We rode over to the neighboring building that housed a licensed funeral lantern manufacturers and ran into Egon Bondy. He couldn't believe his eyes, "what the hell, Vladimír, you're riding a bike, where you off to?" I said: "Hop on the back, Egon, or you can sit on the handlebars, we're going for a health ride." Egon was in a good mood, so he hopped on the back and we turned into Ludmilina Street and then into a passageway where we leaned the bikes against the wall and ordered beer. Mr. Vaništa was beside himself: "What's with the bikes in the passageway? Where are you going?" I said: "The doctor advised us to take frequent bike rides." And Mr. Vaništa: "Where you coming from?" I said: "From Fialas', our place!" Mr. Vaništa screamed: "Today's going to be a shitshow alright!" And suddenly the Rosskopf alarm clock in the passage went off, and Mr. Vaništa heard it and panicked, Bondy with him: "Holy shit, what's that, a fire alarm or something? Fuck me Jesus!" Mr. Vaništa ran out, because the alarm clock was jerking the bikes as it rang and the handlebars were leaving lines and marks in the plaster. So Mr. Vaništa stood there holding the satchel with the ringing alarm clock, holding it as if a time bomb or booby trap were inside. Vladimír calmly opened the satchel and took out the still ringing alarm clock, put it on the beer counter, the two bells ringing so forcefully the clock was in motion . . . Mr. Vaništa took the alarm clock and threw it into the sink, and it was still ringing in the water, just like when you put a mute in a flugelhorn, it kept on ring-ing . . . and Mr. Vaništa laughed himself to tears: "That's a mighty fine piece of gadgetry, no matter how you slice it, old Austria sure was something . . ." When the alarm clock went silent, I pulled it out, dripping water, wound it up, set the hand a little ahead for the alarm to go off, and the clock started ringing with even more verve and louder, I put it back in the satchel, paid, and we walked out to the bikes, Bondy hopped on the rear rack, and we took off on another health ride down the street back home. Egon Bondy regaled us with a wonderful lecture on if God doesn't exist and if no efficient causal ideas exist, then for a modern hero to be typical of the age he must of necessity be a psychopath . . .

One morning Vladimír and I were walking through the Karlín district, and as we were passing by The Green Tree we saw that even though it was summer two sleds were standing in the doorway. We went into the pub. A housepainter was teetering on a stepladder. It was Mr. Nejedlo, who lived in Vaništa's building on the second floor, and like Vladimír he suffered from an asphyxiation complex, and he so loved his drink, and once every three months would hang himself from the door handle right at the moment his wife was coming down the balcony gallery, and she would loosen the rope just in time. He had beautiful brown eyes, like a doe, and he liked us. The beer counter was covered with a cloth splattered with paint, the shelves covered as well, but two old men were sitting at a table, they took up a tiny space at the table and were waiting for the pub to begin service in a couple of hours, toothless both, and because it was summer, they were only in pants and slippers, and each with an open fly, each had on the table two pieces of buttered bread in newspaper, two regulars who'd been languishing for two days while the pub was being painted, but at least they were able to sit there and stare at the cloth covering the beer counter. Mr. Nejedlo said: "Where're you headed?" "Nowhere in particular," we replied, "just wandering," and he called into the kitchen and out came the pubkeeper with bottles of beer for us, and the old men clasped their hands so he brought beer for them as well . . . so we sat with the old men, all of us having a good time, the pubkeeper bringing out bottles of beer, Mr. Nejedlo kept teetering and splattering the old men and us, and the more we were covered in splatters the more stoked Vladimír got and the more detail he went into about the kick he gets out of hanging himself, and he's been doing it since his student days at graphic design school. I kicked him under the table, but Mr. Nejedlo kept his big doe eyes trained on us while rocking on his ladder like a metronome, the paint bespattered old men went to take a piss, still leaving their flies undone, both had apprenticed together and retired as blacksmiths on the same day, both in the same boat, both widowers, in the morning they got their bread buttered at the home and put on the sleds and in the evening pulled the sleds home. "That's the way it should be," Vladimír said approvingly of their confession. And when we'd said goodbye to Mr. Nejedlo, Vladimír told me the painter had such beautiful eyes they were like those of Art Nouveau girls, like the whole of Jugendstil. Three days later Mr. Vaništa invited us to the funeral of a publican. The Association of Publicans Hostimil was burying one of their own and Mr. Vaništa, as a publican, had such a lovely voice, almost like Beniamino Gigli, so we went to the funeral feast at Hotel Splendid, and in the end Mr. Vaništa suggested we all go to his pub and he would play for us a tape of him singing *Adio Mare* and pour us 12° lager from a freshly tapped keg. And when our taxi arrived on Ludmilina Street, the building was open even though it was midnight. Mr. Vaništa jumped out and shouted at the building: "What the heck, the building is wide open for anyone to walk right in and rob me!" He wanted to bolt the door, but morgue workers were bringing down a black coffin on their thin, crooked legs. Vladimír stared unblinking, his head erect, and for the first time even became frightened . . . And a hearse drove up out of the shadow of night and the gleaming coffin was shoved in and the concierge, Mrs. Válečková, formerly a coalwoman, came down the stairs, her eyes still underlined with coal dust, she tottered, stamping down the door catch with the sole of her shoe, and she said: "Láďa, I'm a total wreck . . . you know who they were carrying out? That housepainter Nejedlo. He hung himself on the door handle . . . he thought Růža was coming, but I started talking to her as she was holding the handle while on the other side he was . . . strangling . . . If only I'd known . . ." Mrs. Válečková finished, her hands as big as hockey gloves . . . Vladimír whispered to me: "Doctor, if I shot myself, would you place a hanky under my head?"

One day Egon Bondy agreed to read us some of his prose. For the occasion he bought this stunning red polka-dot cravat, and then he agreed to go with Vladimír for two pails of beer to relax him before reading. So first they brought two pails of beer from Lišeks', then two pails of beer from The Old Post Office. And in the end Bondy agreed to go fetch two pails of beer from Hausmans', because he still wasn't in the right mood to read his prose, his creation, with the proper emphasis. Yet when they got to Hausmans' it was closed. Bondy rapped on the door with a fist, then with both, then with Vladimír joining him they pounded the tin pails on the glass panes, listened, but Mr. Vaništa still didn't open. "Fucking hell," shouted Bondy, "hey, pubkeeper, move your ass, poets have come for beer!" And one blow from a pail knocked out a pane that crashed and cracked on the concrete floor. "Hey, the jewels of the nation have come for beer and you're in there snoring away?" Bondy thundered, and when he bent down to look through the gap of the broken pane into the taproom, the door flew open and Mr. Vaništa ran out in his boxers, a stout, irate publican brandishing a blackjack in his hand, but when he saw Vladimír, whom he liked, he froze with the club cocked in his raised arm, spouting cowhide, the blackjack, a bull's penis stuffed with steel wire. "What do you think you're doing?" Egon Bondy screamed, while Vladimír implored with clasped hands, "you lousy beerman, you dare raise a hand against poets, huh?" screamed Bondy, and Mr. Vaništa was also shouting: "Who's gonna pay for the broken pane, who, who, who, who?" And Egon Bondy commanded: "Get in there and pour us two buckets of beer at once, beer for poets!" and Mr. Vaništa again raised the bullwhip, but Vladimír pleaded with his eyes. "So that's how you're gonna be!" Bondy exploded, "do you know who I am? I'm the poet Egon Bondy!" But Mr. Vaništa: "You can kiss my ass, who's going to pay for that glass pane? Seeing you're a poet, I'll give you one in the piehole!" Bondy roared: "Who? Me? The poet? Hold on now, I'm going to tell the philosopher Zbyněk Fišer about you and he'll give *you* one in the piehole . . . !" and I had already run up and was holding back the blow from the blackjack, that bull's penis stuffed with steel, and I cried: "I'll pay for it, Láďa, he's a poet for real, can't you see that?" And Mr. Vaništa wilted, his red neck went slack, and he lowered the hand holding the blackjack. He smiled and said: "Well, Doctor, a poet, you say? I knew it right away when he smashed the glass pane, well, come on in, boys. Poet, you say? A little high-strung, but who should be more high-strung nowadays than a poet, am I right . . . ?" So on The Levee of Eternity Egon Bondy read to us his beautiful story about Antonín, who crosses the border into Bavaria and all the tribulations he experiences in twenty-four hours. Twice more we went out to fill the pails with beer, and only after all his ordeals did Antonín run in jubilation toward the cottage he saw before him, thinking it was Bavarian but then realizing it was the very same cottage he'd left in Bohemia. And Egon Bondy became terrified that all the pubs would be closed and we would be left to suffer in our thirst, so he woke up the lady on the ground floor, where there used to be a clothes mangle, and borrowed from her a jug and a bucket and all three of us went out to buy enough beer to fill them. When we had drunk everything and Egon Bondy was walking with his head erect, as if his back were in a cast, so that none of the beer would spill out of him, only then did he agree to let us accompany him to the tram stop. And as we were waiting on the main street, Bondy fell backward and his head forcefully banged against shutters and slid down them. Behind these shutters were the offices of the SNB, the national police, and out ran two officers and a sergeant in an unbuttoned jacket. Bondy was lying on his back, they helped him to sit up, and all thirty pages of the manuscript about Antonín walking across the border were strewn over the ground like lottery tickets. Horrified, Vladimír and I didn't make a peep, but Egon Bondy: "Dammit all, Sarge, are you blind! Pick up those pages for me, my text, for Christ's sake, get moving before a tram runs them over, fuck me Jesus!" And the young cops picked up the pages about Antonín who wanted to leave his native land for hostile Bavaria, and as they were handing him the pages the sergeant glanced a moment at the text, his eyes scanning almost an entire page, and he nodded, and when the nearly empty tram slowly pulled up, he motioned with his chin and the young cops helped Egon Bondy into the tram, and as he rode off Bondy began to sing, shaking the pages the sergeant had given him tightly clutched in his fingers: "No one knows about me, that I'm a Marxist lefty . . ." And the sergeant said: "Both hands in his case . . ." and he motioned for the two young cops to slip back into the warm office, and on the last step he turned around to us and said, given how downcast we looked: "Good thing no one from the police read that. Good night!" And the shutters loudly clattered as he pulled them down. Vladimír said: "All in all that Egon Bondy is a delightful, plucky little fellow, he sure served us up an enjoyable evening . . . but I'm about to puke, Doctor, what about you . . . ?"

When he lived on The Levee of Eternity, Vladimír wore glasses, and for that matter he wore glasses later as well . . . but he used these glasses more as a lorgnette. When something was worthy of his closer attention he would use the spectacles folded as they were . . . like some certified handwriting expert or a philatelist . . . he liked to wear glasses that were missing something, either a lens or more often one of the temples. Sometimes Vladimír accentuated his natural charm by using wire to reconnect glasses broken in two, other times he replaced a missing temple with string attached to the end piece, which sometimes was a knot closely cut with scissors or a piece of string hanging down nearly to his chin . . . yet whatever the case, they were always rigged in a way that was visually striking, to look good on him . . . For that matter, no one ever found Vladimír to be anything other than visually striking, sculptural, like a roebuck or a wildcat in nature . . .

When Vladimír had his second wedding in Český Krumlov on August 22, 1968, I was invited to be his witness. But imagine my surprise when I set out in the car that I could not get out of Prague, not by driving through the center nor by driving through the outskirts, because fraternal armies had shown up to quash something that didn't exist. So I returned home and went to an exhibition at the Wallenstein Riding School, I knocked on the gates, but the exhibition had been postponed on account of the arrival of these armies. When Egon Bondy heard about this, he screamed: "Fuck me Jesus! That Vladimír! Will it ever be my luck to have so many armies set in motion by my wedding? The only grandiose thing to have happened to me was when I asked you to give Rudi Dutschke my regards, and when you entered his building to deliver these salutations they were right then carrying him out with a bullet in his head. But five armies on the move to prevent a wedding, this is on an entirely different level, I'll never be mixed up in something like this! And why not? Because Vladimír has always attracted great events and misfortunes. Just the way it is. Fuck me Jesus, he's got all the luck!"

We were sitting with friends in The Tomcat, right across from the taps, Vladimír next to Karel Marysko, the poet, who in the 1950s showed up one day at The Levee of Eternity with three suitcases and moved in with us. He slept behind the kitchen stove off to the side because he was always cold. More than a dozen times Vladimír wanted to wipe him out for no other reason than each time they were together Marysko always asked him the same question: "Do you know how to paint a hand?" And each time Vladimír would get so angry he would be sharpening the hatchet with a file beneath our windows . . . but today when Marysko asked: "Do you know how to paint a hand?" Vladimír only smiled . . . So we sat with friends in comity in The Tomcat, Mr. Čihák, who had come over from The Golden Tiger, poured a fantastically smooth beer, when the door opened, a hand pulled back the red curtain, and into the pub stepped Forman, the movie director, accompanied by his assistant, Ivan Passer. And when the celebrated director set his eyes on our table, he began to wildly exclaim: "Painmaker, painmaker, painmaker! Painmaker!" And he looked at Vladimír in the corner and again shouted: "Remember? The painmaker! Come on! A red-hot hook over my knuckles!" And all of us looked over at Vladimír in admiration, what sort of marvelous happening was again in the offing for us in The Tomcat, but he couldn't remember, he simply stood up, extended his hand, and Forman came over to the table, shook Vladimír's hand, and looked at Marysko, the poet, hunched over next to Vladimír under the weight of sexual and erotic issues, and Forman sat down, put a hand on the poet's shoulder, and to our table as well as to all the neighboring tables began to ecstatically explain: "You're Mr. Marysko, aren't you? Yes, it's you! During the Protectorate didn't you teach music in Čáslav? Yes, you did! Well I was one of your students, ten-year-old Miloš Forman! Gentlemen! Every time we were practicing scales Mr. Marysko here would gently rap us with an oak cane he called the painmaker. Yes, the painmaker! And I once told you: Teacher, sir, I'm playing so poorly because it's cold in here! And Mr. Marysko replied: All right, Forman, now go to the window and tell me what you see. I looked out the window onto the square and said: Teacher, sir, I see a statue of the patriot Pastor Matouš Ulický. And Mr. Marysko: All right, Forman, and what stands out on this statue? And I said: Teacher, sir, he has no hands, the enemy cut them off. And Mr. Marysko exclaimed: All right, Forman, and if you continue to play like you've been playing, that's how you're going to end up . . . so get on with practice, a burning painmaker is at the ready! And as I played the scales, Mr. Marysko pulled a red-hot hook from the stove and held it over my fingers and roared: If you're cold, you need to keep your knuckles warm, nice and warm . . . !" Forman told this to all present and everyone was all worked up, roaring with laughter and congratulating Marysko, who straightened up with all the glory directed at him, and no one had noticed that

Vladimír was still standing, his hand still extended from when Forman pulled away his hand, gazing into the heart of ruination, then he paid, no one noticing him, and he left, the peals of boisterous laughter and cries of Painmaker! Painmaker! Painmaker! nipping at his heels through the door. When Egon Bondy, who just had eight teeth extracted on the dentist's whim, heard about this, he rejoiced: "Hahahahaha! Finally! Finally! Finally! Finally that poetic surreality has turned off its spigot of the marvelous, it has finally abandoned Vladimír, his victorious hahahaha has finally run its course!" Bondy rejoiced with his swollen cheeks, but as soon as he finished he said in a voice marked by malign foreboding: "This would've brought me such joy ten years ago, but today I don't feel any joy because what happened in The Tomcat is just the timpani of an overture, and not just to the symphony of Vladimír's fate but the percussion to my lachrymose, salubrious, melancholic imagination as well . . . because Vladimír and I, we're the two focal points of the same ellipse, two coupled axles . . . we're a bonded and registered company like Wichterle & Kovářík, like Lauren & Klement . . . Ayayayay!" Bondy moaned and clasped his delicate white hands and waved them overhead in the black air of Bonaparte's, and throwing back his head he softly whimpered, then to demonstrate his Galician sorrow with gestures as brisk and rapid as an orchestra conductor, in one swift motion he ripped out all the buttons of his coat lapels and dumped an ashtray full of smoldering cigarette butts on his head . . . and his beautiful hair, greasy with melancholy, caught fire and the customers had to put it out with beer. "Fuck me Jesus," Egon bellowed under his breath, "that urchin Vladimír is at the root of all this!"

The morning after the night it happened to Vladimír I saw Dr. Drvota, the psychiatrist, fly up the courtyard stairs, and I could see from afar the grief in his eyes, he jiggled the handle, then knocked on the window, his hands forming a brim over his eyes so he could better see through the glass if I was at home. I was standing in the doorway Vladimír and I had bricked up and then unbricked years ago, standing in the shadows, my heart pounding, then I saw the psychiatrist's back move away, the director of the crisis hotline receding, just a bust, then just a head, and finally the hat passed from sight . . . I lay on the floor and listened to bygone times return with so much color and vibrancy, time rounded out by a tunnel back to where it began when I first met Vladimír on Old Town Square as I washed myself at four a.m. in the fountain with the fish, and he was doing the same, that broken tunnel when we didn't see one another only to meet again and pick back up the thread to continue what and where we had left off, lying on my back on the carpet I saw the tunnel's end, but straightening out, and that night Vladimír had taken off for the Cosmos from a launchpad he'd prepared long ago and for which he'd practiced and trained . . . Again someone was banging on my window like crazy, and then on the door, and back to the window, alternating like discordant timpani, through the curtains I saw the dazed, ashen face of Vladimír's cousin, bristling in terror and horror, and this confirmed for me on the other side that Vladimír had definitively met his end, and I realized that I couldn't get up, that I could only lie on my back and stare unblinking at the ceiling . . . And then the cousin raced down the stairs, my eyes helping to push her into the background, then came a long silence, the sun slid across the high courtyard wall, dazzling, solemn . . . and Egon Bondy ran into this sun, he gave the window and locked door a hostile look, then he, too, started to knock and call, then he heard the silence, and he ran into the middle of the courtyard, turned around, raised his delicate outspread hands and offered his palms and arteries to the sun, and throwing back his bearded, hairy head, now replete with halo, scented and sparkling with Pilsner and flush with ecstasy, like Doctor Ecstaticus, he cried out: "*Mein gutester Herr Vladimír!* The bell has tolled for phenomenological angst, now you can say so long to having to adapt, no need to bother with existence or imagination or transcendence anymore, no need to care about metaphysics anymore. *Mister Vladimír!* You're flying straight to where the essence of things inhuman as well as indispensable to humanity are found. My farewell to you is only for a moment, because my solace is also mere ontology, an invisible yet very real kingdom into which you now enter in a rocket far more powerful than Apollo 12! No need to go into orbit first, you're flying without a transfer ticket, direct by way of grace, just like an intervention by the ancient God, now dead. *Monsieur Vladimír!* I see you flying on your back, zipped up in the fly of ontology, right into the very center of an equilateral triangle, right into the heart, into the switchboard of being . . . ! *Panie Wladimirze! Panie Wladimirze! Panie Wladimirze!*" "What's with all this racket, all this hollering is wrecking my kid's sleep!" Mrs. Slavíčková shouted down from the balcony, a good mother. "You'll give my little Jenda the shakes again!" And she was right, the glorious truth of a protective mother, just as Vladimír was right in the truth of those artists who came before us, just as I was right, lying there inert, paralyzed by grief, on the floor of my room, just as Egon Bondy, transformed into Zbyněk Fišer, was right when he thundered his truth from the launchpad of the courtyard on The Levee of Eternity in Libeň . . .

LETTER TO THOSE ATTENDING A VERNISSAGE

You who are reading this text, all of you who are looking at Vladimír's prints, don't just think about his modus operandi as an artist, don't analyze what Vladimír wanted his prints to say about reality, while you look at them think about the radiance and marvelousness of reality, ticking from one second to the next, on and on into eternity. Think about Vladimír, who felt at home wherever he was, think about the fact that his studio was always where he was at that moment, think about his eyes, at once childlike and scientific, attentively observing the spherical surface around him in such a way as to lend what seemed trivial and insignificant, what others despised, a deplorable grandeur and monumental beauty, even if the surface was no larger than a handkerchief. All of you who aspire to become visual artists, don't wait until you have a studio, and are in Prague, know that Vladimír's studio was so small that if three people were in it the fourth had to stand in the hallway . . . and yet in that Žižkov cubbyhole of his he achieved a greatness with his active prints on par with what Pollock and Mathieu achieved with action painting. You, who are merely spectators, all of you, try to emulate Vladimír and pull back the skin of matter, aspire to reach the beautiful mucosae of animate and inanimate forms, don't be afraid to perform a vivisection on yourselves, or on anything, because only in this way, until your dying day, will you be able to feast with wonder on the knowledge that matter created human eyes only so that it could locate and recognize in them its own manifold beauty. All of you who are looking at Vladimír's prints, know that he was trained as a lathe operator, that he loved all the means of expression such work and materials offered, by which and with which

useful objects and components are created, that he understood absolutely everything associated with the concept of machine shop, that at some point he was
able to creatively apply all of it to his printmaking such that no other graphic artist
created such protean, magnificent, exquisite artifacts as did he. His active prints
electrify the art aesthetician and the metalsmith both, and they hold up under
the shrewdest intellectual scrutiny as well as the most acute sensuous scrutiny. All
of you who are looking at Vladimír's prints, know that I was also startled by his
ability to immediately notice materials and events I did not see. A smile of aston-
ishment always appeared on his face whenever he encountered the marvelous, and
then I would walk in the direction his eyes were pointing and keep going . . . until I
saw it! And always it was metal filings and sawdust, an overturned truck with
dried asphalt, dust covering wood beams, the blast furnace at the Poldi steel mill, a
bird carrying a blade of grass for nest building . . . In general, rather ordinary
marvels and the marvelous were always fast friends with Vladimír. Having drunk
our beer and making our way home above Vysočany, we sat for awhile with the
trains rumbling beneath us, and Vladimír surveyed the lumps of rough sand under
his shoes and observed, as if from Skylab overhead, whole mountain ranges and
huge alpine mountains, and he quietly related everything he saw on Earth, the
stunning Alps and Pyrenees; his shoe lumped some sand together and he continued his ascent of the Andes and the Himalayas without leaving the Vysočany
hillside. When we were swimming in a channel of the river at Libeň, Vladimír
often sat on the last step and let the waves wash over his feet and explain that
he saw no reason to travel around the world when he could sail the Black Sea and
the Atlantic Ocean right here in Libeň with no less brio than Rimbaud's when he
wrote *The Drunken Boat* while sitting curled up at the bottom of a barge. You
would never find Vladimír in the more famous pubs like The Golden Tiger or The
Two Cats or Pinkas' or Schnells'. Whenever I went looking for him I had to follow
a route leading from one pub to the next as if they were accoutrements to his poetics. If he wasn't at The Tram Stop in Vysočany, then I went to Čížeks', and if he
wasn't there, then on to The Chestnut Tree, and if he wasn't there then a sliver of

hope remained that he would be drinking 10° lager while standing at The Russian Court, and if he wasn't there either, then I would have to hop on a tram and look for him in Žižkov at The Rosebush, and when told no one had seen him for two days, then I knew for sure I would find him at dusk either at Gradmothers' or sitting in The Knight of Malvasia operating the record player. Sometimes he was at Hausmans' on Ludmilina Street in Libeň or one street over at Přemysl's . . . and always these pubs had the lovely smell of spilled beer and tablecloths full of calamities from spilled coffee and liquor, and it goes without saying they all had to have godawful bathrooms, naturally with pipes aesthetically rusted and lovely waterfalls of crusty tar embellished with canary yellow piss stains, such that Vladimír often stood staring into the runnel of the urinal trough at matches and cigarette butts decorated with disinfectant balls and slices of lemon, crowing about how beautiful it all was and if he had the strength and artistic skill he would run this whole tar wall through the etching press and print it onto paper. Once Vladimír and I were leaving The Blue Star, and when we crossed over to the sidewalk, he froze, thunderstruck. And I saw that joyous smile of amazement again appear on his face, and again I was envious and taken aback that he was seeing something I'd walked past ages ago and never noticed. When I found the strength to follow the direction of his eyes, I saw at the end of his gaze giant tin letters mounted all the way up near the gable of a four-story building, emotionally charged letters forming the word KRÁSA, that is, "beauty." I realized at once this was the last remnant of fame of Czech philosopher Ladislav Klíma, who had once lived in Hotel Krása, and so Vladimír and I agreed that he would lend me a pair of overalls and first thing the next day we would take down the letters and put them up in the Red shrine at the ČKD plant, and if they refused, then we would give them to the Mánes Association of Artists. So we showed up the next day and couldn't believe our eyes. When we inquired inside about the sign, we were told that workmen from the property office had taken the letters down and hauled them off to the scrapyard, because that KRÁSA, that beauty, was a public hazard that could fall on passersby . . . So again, all of you who are looking at Vladimír's prints, know that he was not disappointed, nor did he berate anyone or curse the workmen, he just smiled the whole evening and kept silent, actually delighted the workmen had given us a punchline to such a lovely story. And we made the rounds of the pubs and waited for some other conspiracy and act of malice to deliver reality to us. Again we were standing in the World Cafeteria, drinking superb beer, and again I saw that smile on Vladimír's face, and it had to be something intense at the end of his gaze because the surge of reality became too much for him and he had to lower his eyes. When he regained his composure, he again trained his eyes on a spot over my shoulder, as if he couldn't believe what he were seeing, but this time he maintained eye contact with something in the passageway leading to the World Cinema. Vladimír always looked at objects and events that fell in the purview of his poetics just as if he were smitten and making eyes at a beautiful woman whose eyes were admiring him in return. I turned around to see what he was looking at and saw a Gypsy girl etching scribble with a pin into the painted glass wall . . . Vladimír grabbed two pints of beer and we went out to the passage, and what we saw gave us a jolt. The glass clattered against his teeth when he took a swig, so extravagant was this gigantic image etched by thousands of human hands into the exterior of a glass wall painted white, which children and lovers, moviegoers, had over several years, by coin or knife, pin or lipstick edge, entirely covered with signs and symbols, initials and messages, much of it just random scrawl, like when you absentmindedly doodle in the margins of a newspaper or school exercise book . . . Vladimír spread his arms still holding the pint of beer and declared that as soon as we found the money we'd buy that pane of glass, the window of the World Cafeteria's storeroom, and take that beauty home. And yes, we scrounged up a thousand crowns and came the next day, at the threshold of the passageway Vladimír already let out his victorious laugh: Hahahahaaa! When we walked up to the World Cafeteria's storeroom, a painter was kneeling and meticulously graining and daubing the last scribbles with paint and the whole glass wall was white like a canvas primed and readied as a tabula rasa for everything to begin anew. All of you who are looking at Vladimír's prints, know that such anecdotes can happen to you, too, I believe, if you were to imbue them with the portent of a marvelous encounter, if you were to consider your life as singular, and therefore beautiful. All it takes is the courage to leap head first into the irreversible present to find yourself at once in the very heart of eternity. I remember when Vladimír and I took a trip to Pikovice to visit his aunt. But when we got off the train and saw the swollen, turbid Sázava, it didn't even take a minute for its allure to grab us, and we stripped in silence, one followed the other into the current of late spring floodwaters, and we were carried off with the speed of a bicycle racer, the hills and roads rushing backward, and Vladimír was again fired up and beautiful, and when the swollen current rumbled us with increasing speed over the place where normally a weir would be, Vladimír shouted: Hahahaaaa . . . ! When the river had carried us more than a kilometer from our clothes it deposited us in a still pool . . . and we walked back against the current to do the whole marvelous ride over again. Vladimír only regretted that it wasn't made even more exquisite by getting a small gash in his thigh from a nail when hurtling over the weir so he could experience Alberto Burri being the first to intentionally slash the surface of an exhibited painting. He can't want everything, he added, it's enough to have the experience of one of his plates being spit out on the other side by the sluice of the press's rollers. This was a glorious period when Vladimír knew how to compress an experience into a print that would express it. Around this time Vladimír and I rode a motorcycle to Nymburk. I couldn't go any faster than my Jawa 250 Pérák was able, but Vladimír liked to tell folks how we zipped down forest paths through Elbian dunes and went into a skid. I remember Vladimír flying over me headfirst into a thicket and so engulfed in it only his shoes were visible. Horrified, I circled the thicket as I called, "My God, Vladimír, are you okay?" I found him in the sand with a lump on his forehead, but howling with laughter and pumped that I had prepared such a wonderful Sunday for him, and inspired by this tumble into the thicket he would make a series of prints for me. Yet the most spectacular series of monotypes, nearly thirty-five large-format prints created during the last period of his work, was thanks to a Jawa 500 driven by Kotrč, a lathe operator who came with Vladimír, sitting in the tiny sidecar as if he were in a sitz bath, to visit me in Nymburk. Because of the impression this one ride made on him, and a minor loan, Vladimír worked two days only for Mr. Kotrč with the condition that Kotrč would buy him inks and for 48 hours keep him supplied with pitchers of beer. Mr. Kotrč was a small man, taciturn, meek, and he had an awful row with his wife just to be able to hang on the wall . . . only one of those thirty-five gems. All of you who are looking at Vladimír's prints, know that albeit a proletarian he was an aristocrat whose life is worthy of emulation by those who still think life should be lived to the full.

Vladimír's experiments on himself that skirted the boundary between life and death had enormous consequences . . . for Vladimír. He was perpetrator, victim, and judge all wrapped into one. The more the opposition between life and death could be dissolved the more a higher synthesis of antitheses could be created, and this would present the opportunity to live at the expense of oneself alone and the universe. An introverted class struggle, an introverted exploitation of only oneself . . . and the result is Vladimír's mighty laugh and manic bliss suddenly becoming melancholic sorrow and Heraclitean weeping, which in turn are plat-forms for the reemergence of joy, the Great Yes from the Great No. Through this rhythmic dying and rising from the dead, Vladimír is the symbol of the pantheistic Demiurge, the Creator in the image of God whom Egon Bondy claimed died long ago . . .

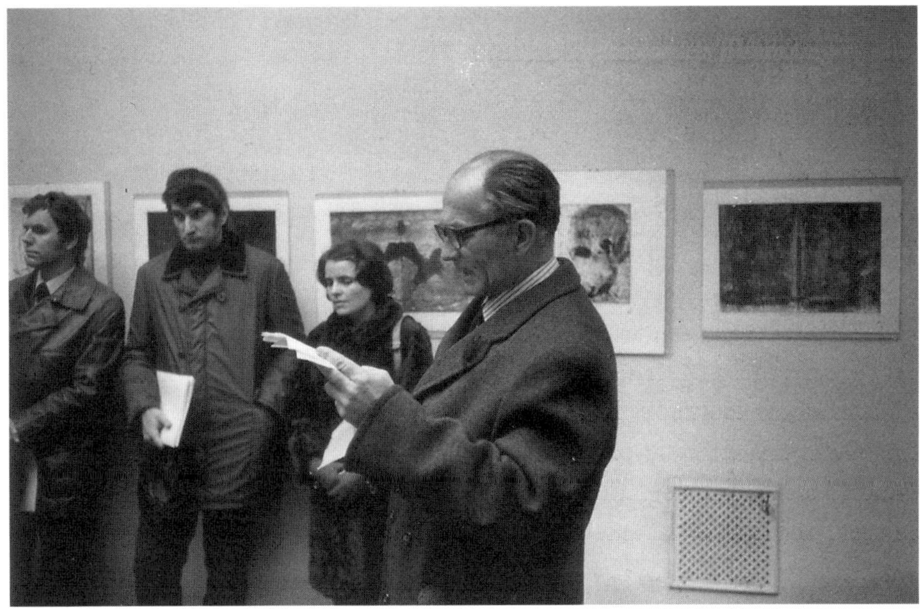

Bohumil Hrabal reading "Letter to Those Attending a Vernissage" at the opening of the Boudník exhibition (in the background) at Galerie pod radnicí in Ústí nad Orlicí on January 26, 1974.

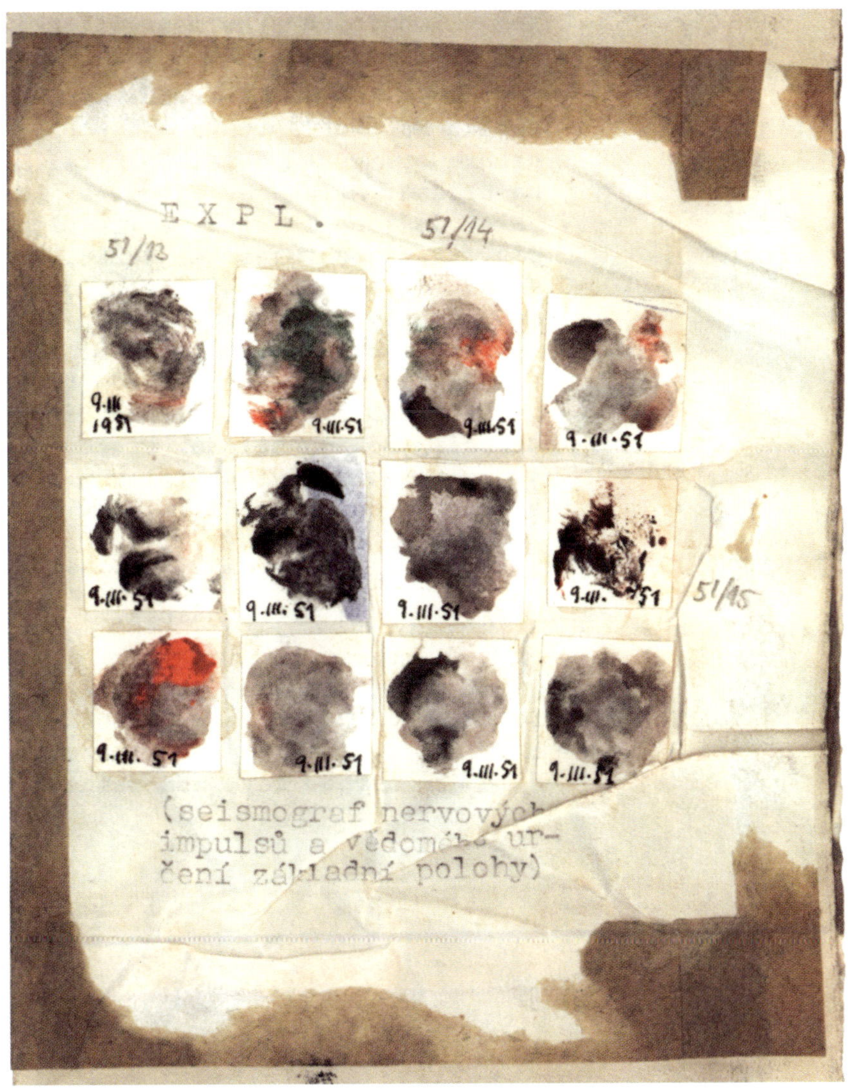

Explosionalist blotches, "Seismograph of nerve impulses and conscious determination of primary position," 1951

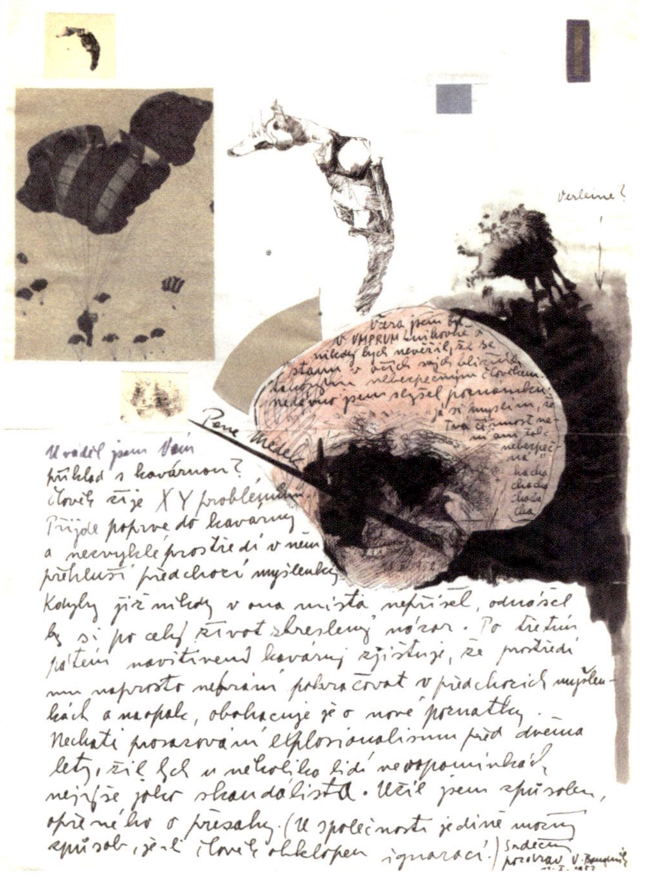

Letter of January 11, 1952

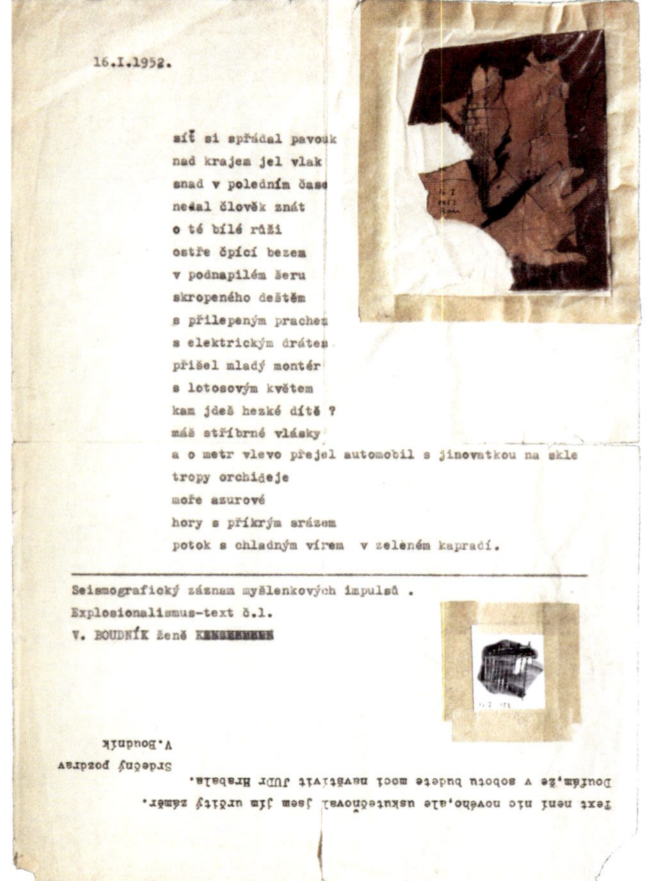

16.I.1952.

síť si spřádal pavouk
nad krajem jel vlak
snad v poledním čase
nedal člověk znát
o té bílé růži
ostře čpící bezem
v podnapilém šeru
skropeného deštěm
s přilepeným prachem
s elektrickým drátem
přišel mladý montér
s lotosovým květem
kam jdeš hezké dítě ?
máš stříbrné vlásky
a o metr vlevo přejel automobil s jinovatkou na skle
tropy orchideje
moře azurové
hory s příkrým srázem
potok s chladným vírem v zeleném kapradí.

Seismografický záznam myšlenkových impulsů .
Explosionalismus-text č.1.
V. BOUDNÍK ženě

V.Boudník
Srdečný pozdrav
Doufám,že v sobotu budete moci navštívit JUDr Hrabala.
text není nic nového,ale skutečňoval jsem jím určitý záměr.

Letter of January 16, 1952, "Seismograms of thought impulses. Explosionalism – text no. 1."

Explosionalist letters to Mikuláš Medek, pen, collage, blots in India ink

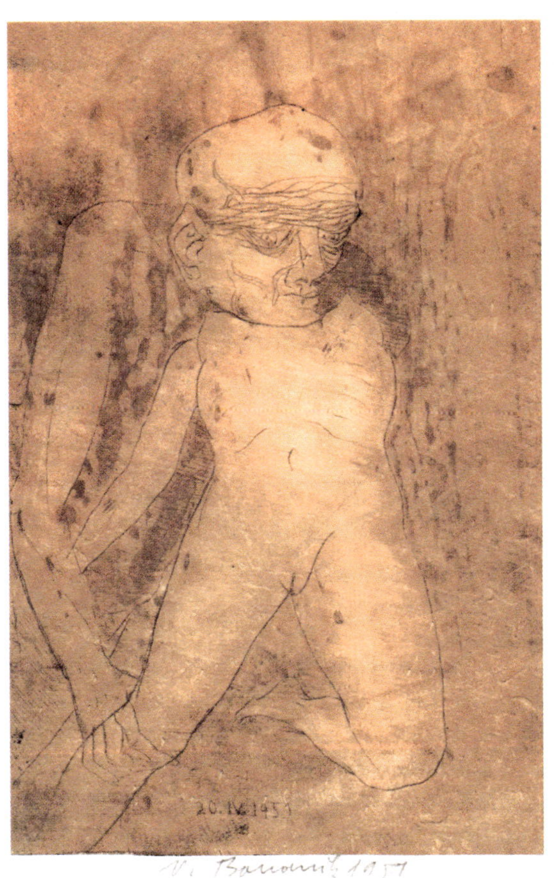

Untitled, drypoint, 1951

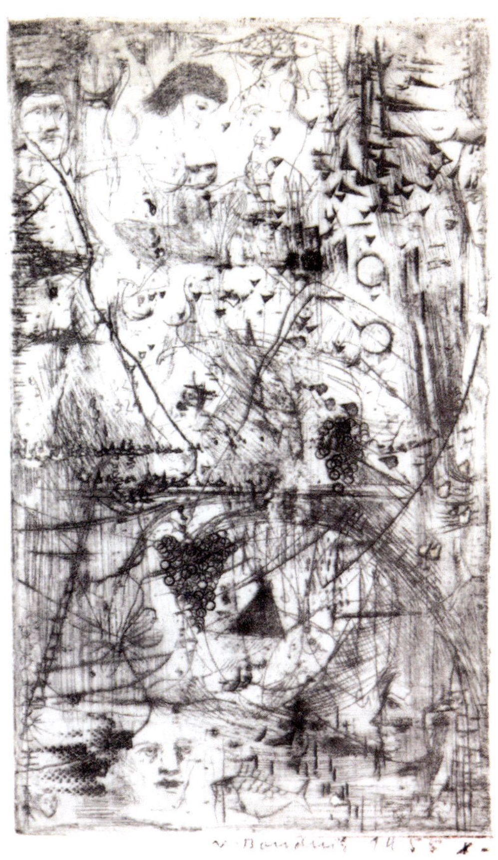

Memories, Bildsalat, drypoint & active print, 1955

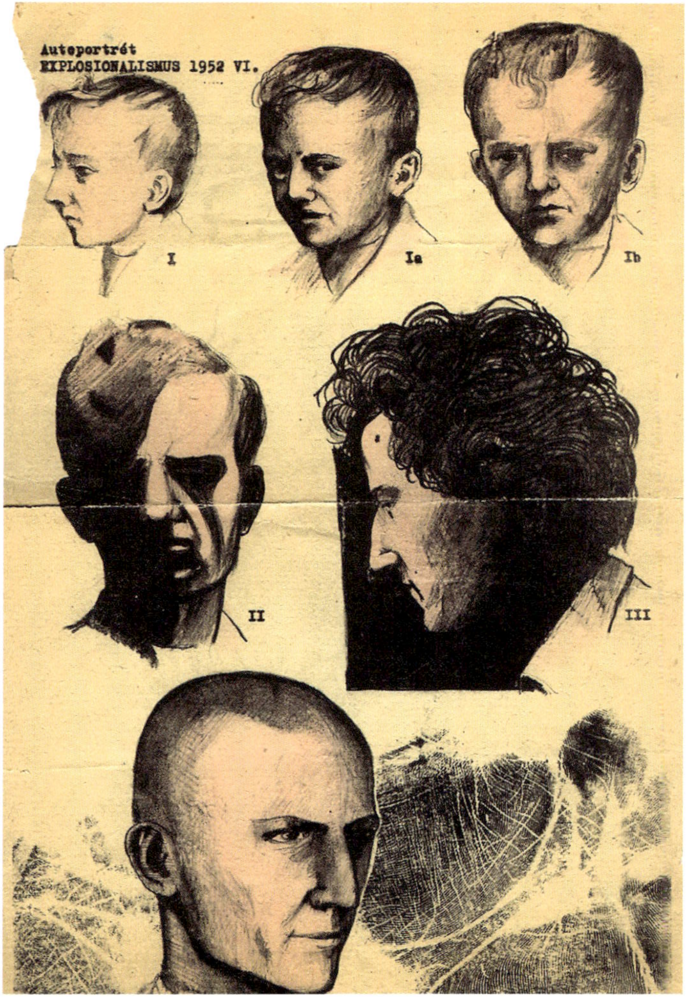

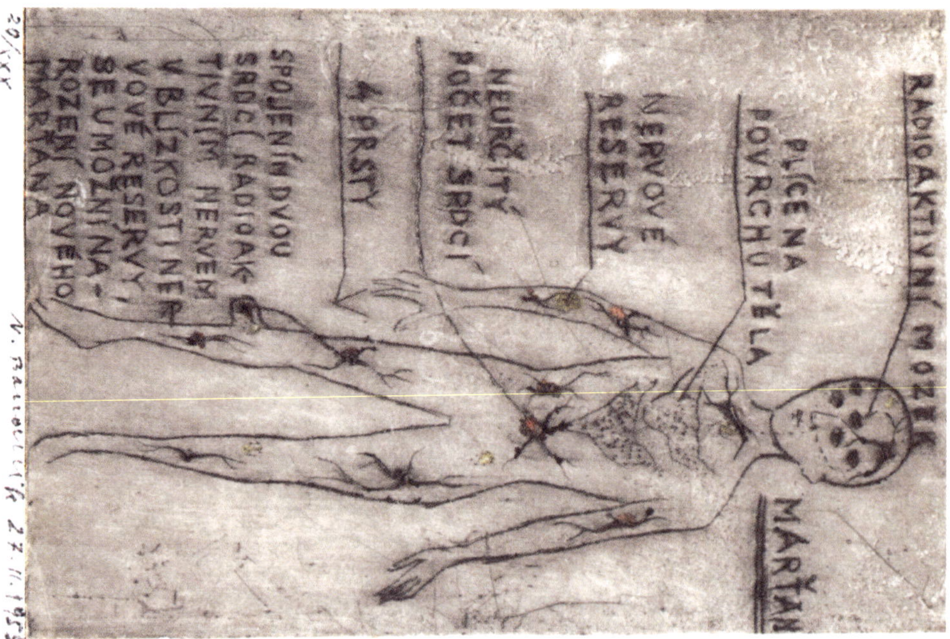

Self-portrait, Explosionalism, offset lithography on paper, hand-colored, 1952

Martian (with radioactive brain, indeterminate number of hearts, etc.), drypoint & active print, 1955

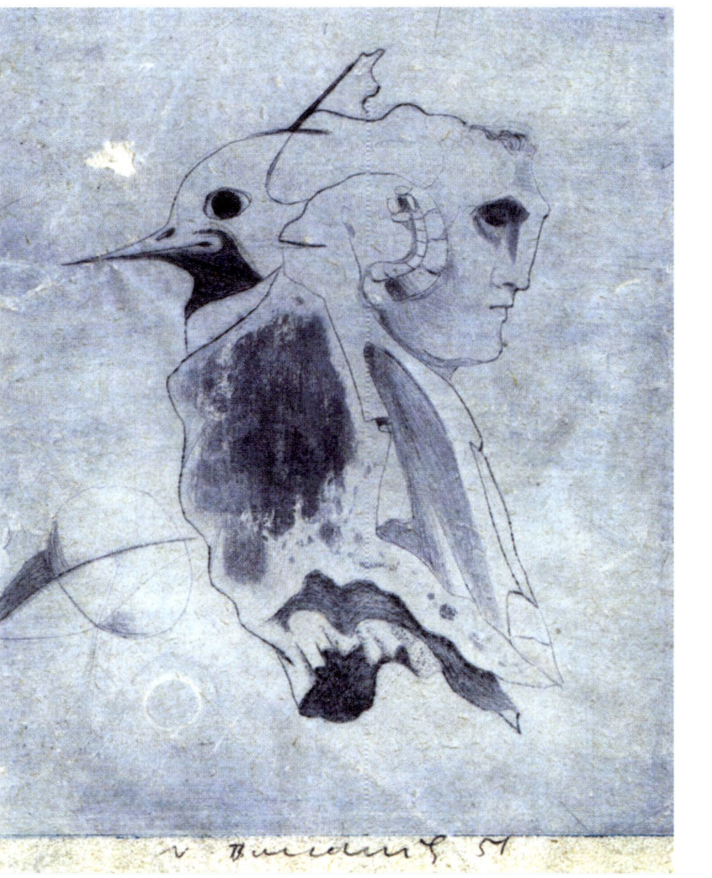

Man-Bird Triple Portrait, aquatint & drypoint, 1951

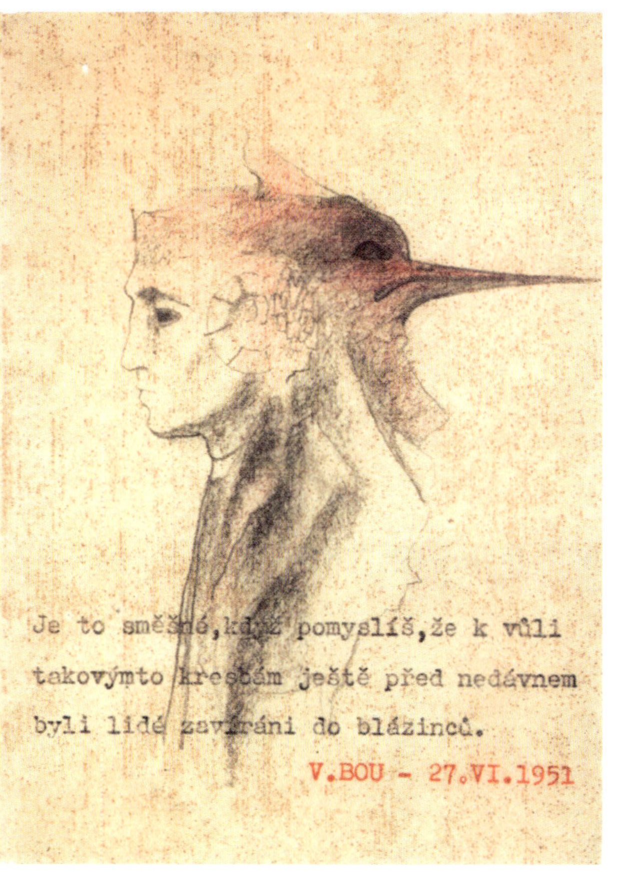

Man-Bird, drawing in pencil and pastel, "It's absurd when you think about it, but drawings such as this got folks thrown into the madhouse not so long ago," 1951

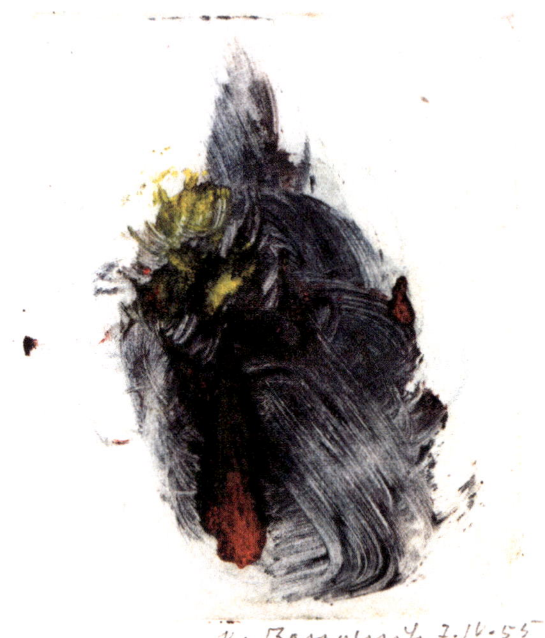

Orchids, monotype, 1955

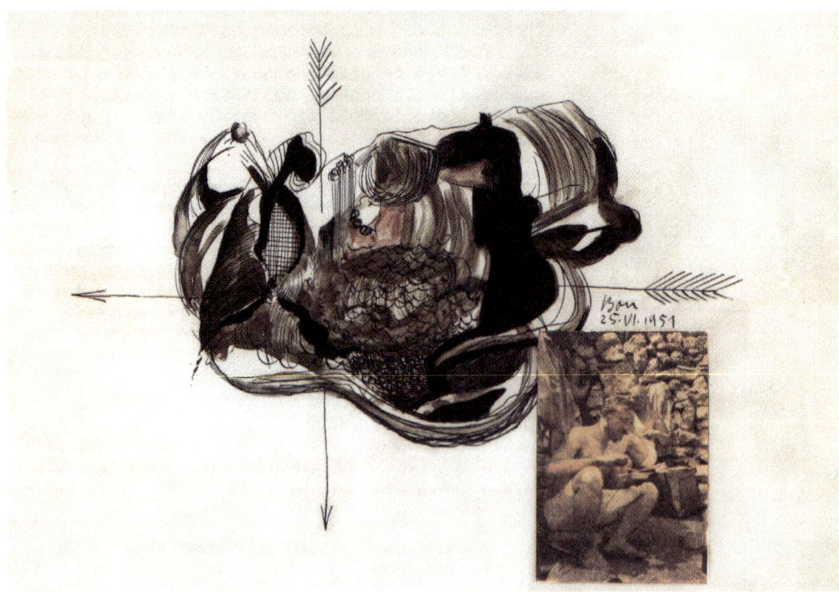

Collage : pen and ink, watercolor, photograph, 1951

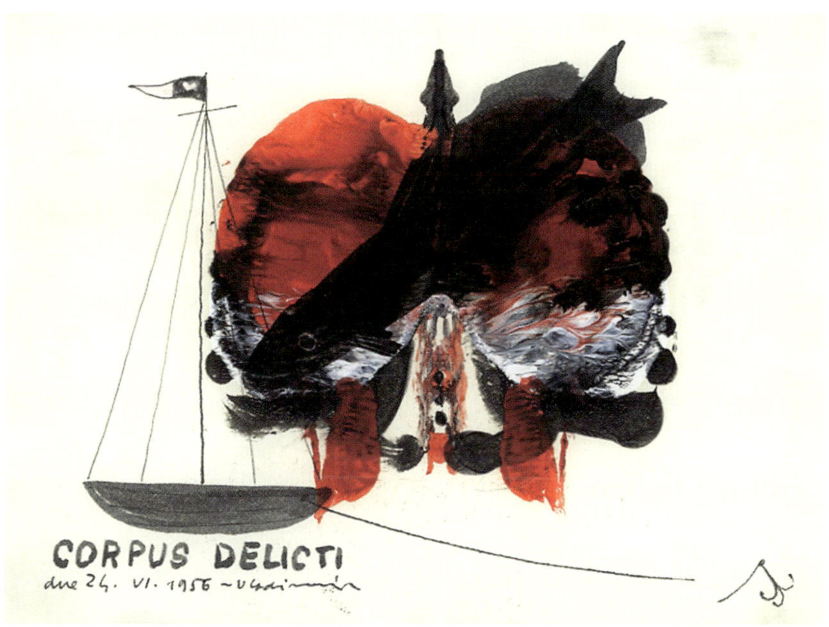

Corpus Delecti, Explosionalist Editions, car paint & India ink on paper, 1956

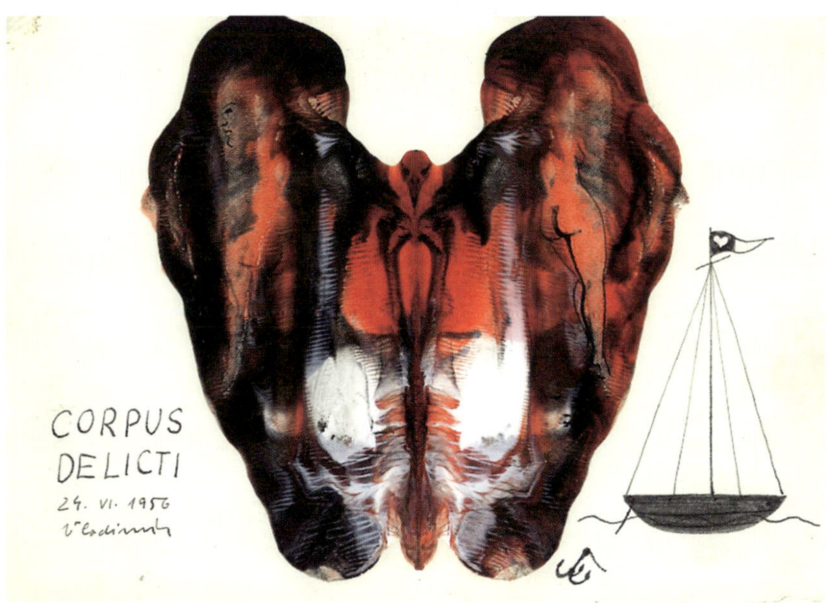

Corpus Delecti, Explosionalist Editions, car paint & India ink on paper, 1956

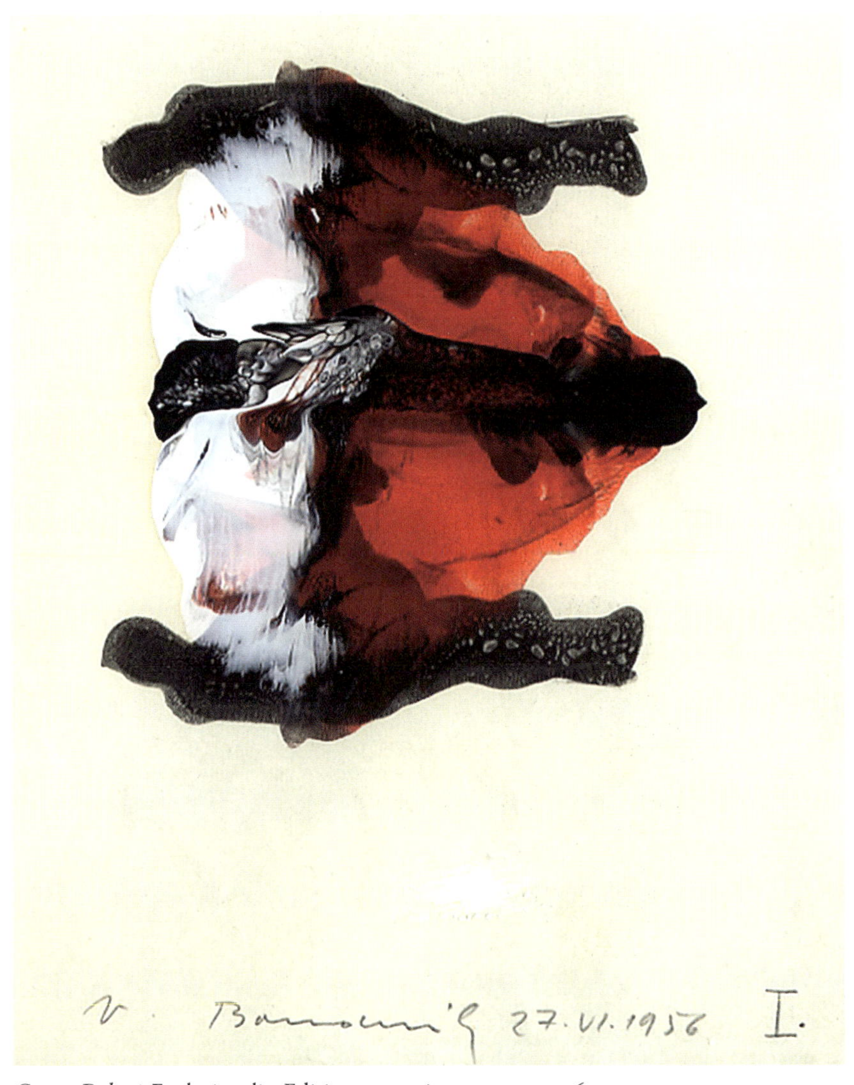

Corpus Delecti, Explosionalist Editions, car paint on paper, 1956

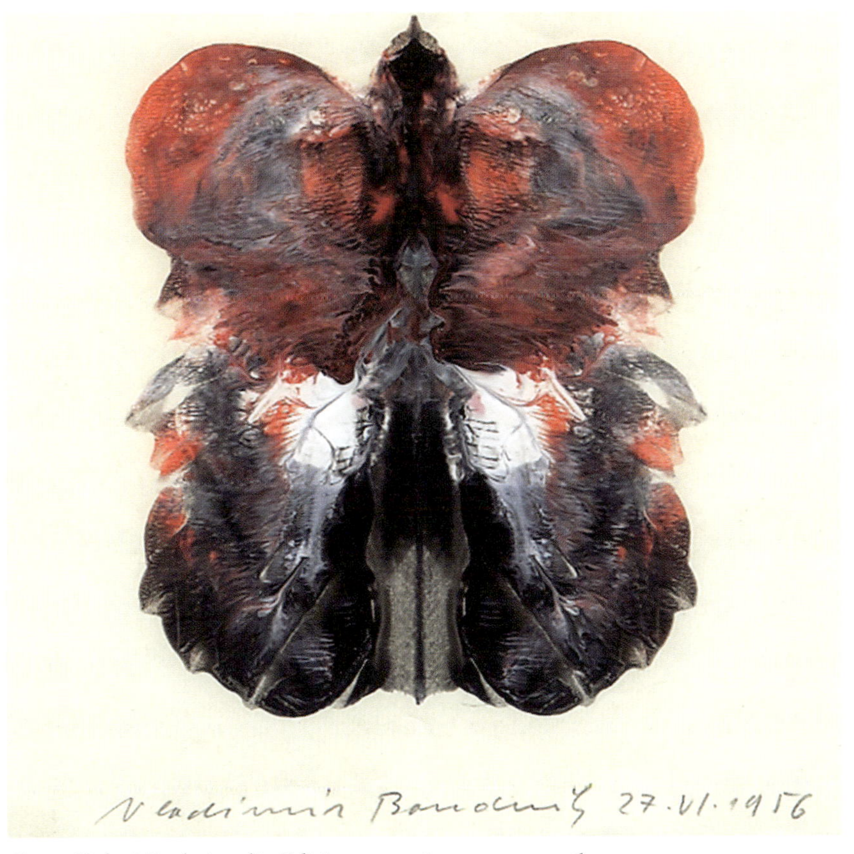

Corpus Delecti, Explosionalist Editions, car paint on paper, 1956

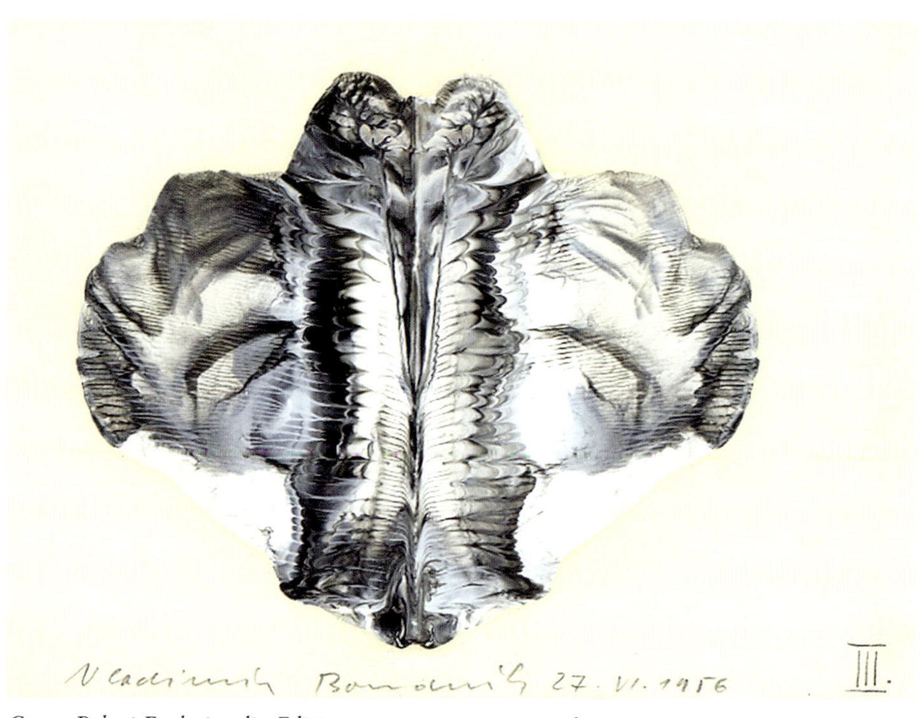

Corpus Delecti, Explosionalist Editions, car paint on paper, 1956

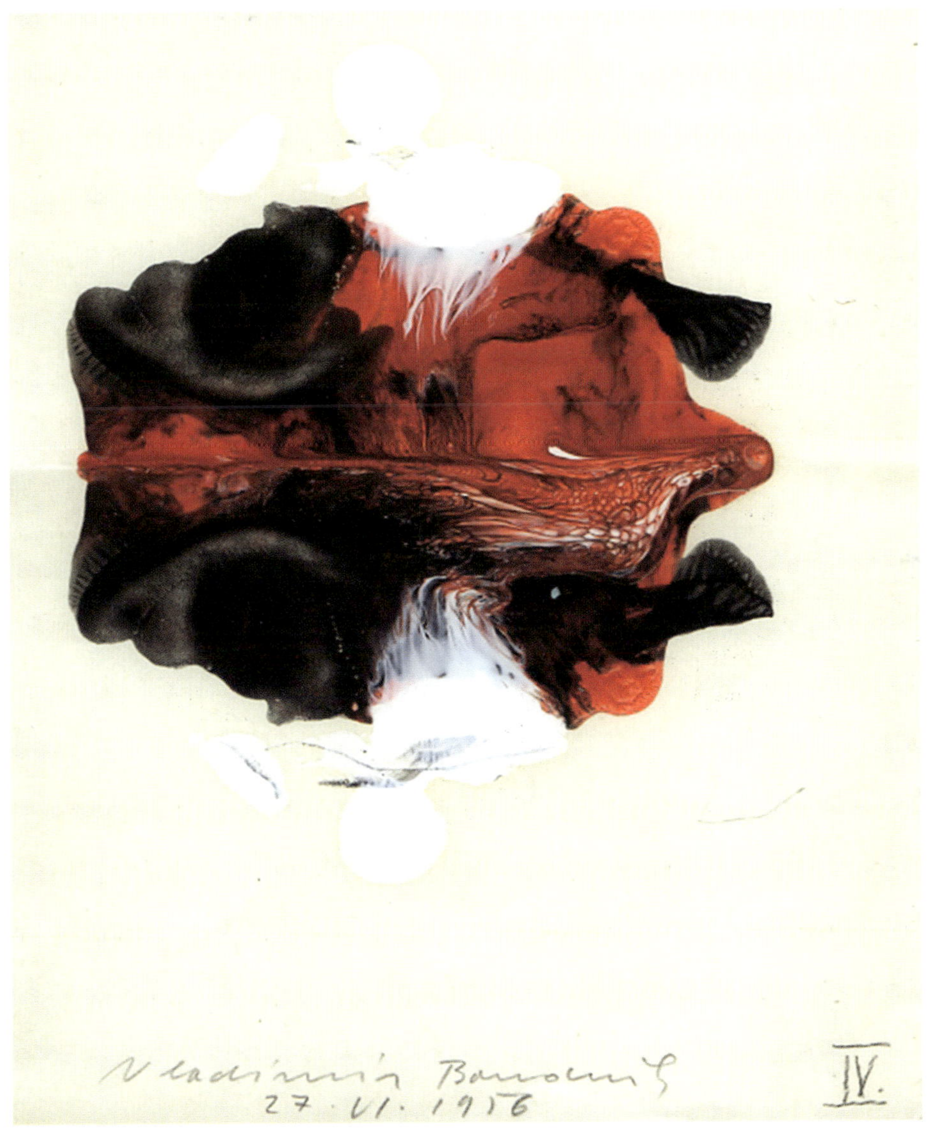

Corpus Delecti, Explosionalist Editions, car paint on paper, 1956

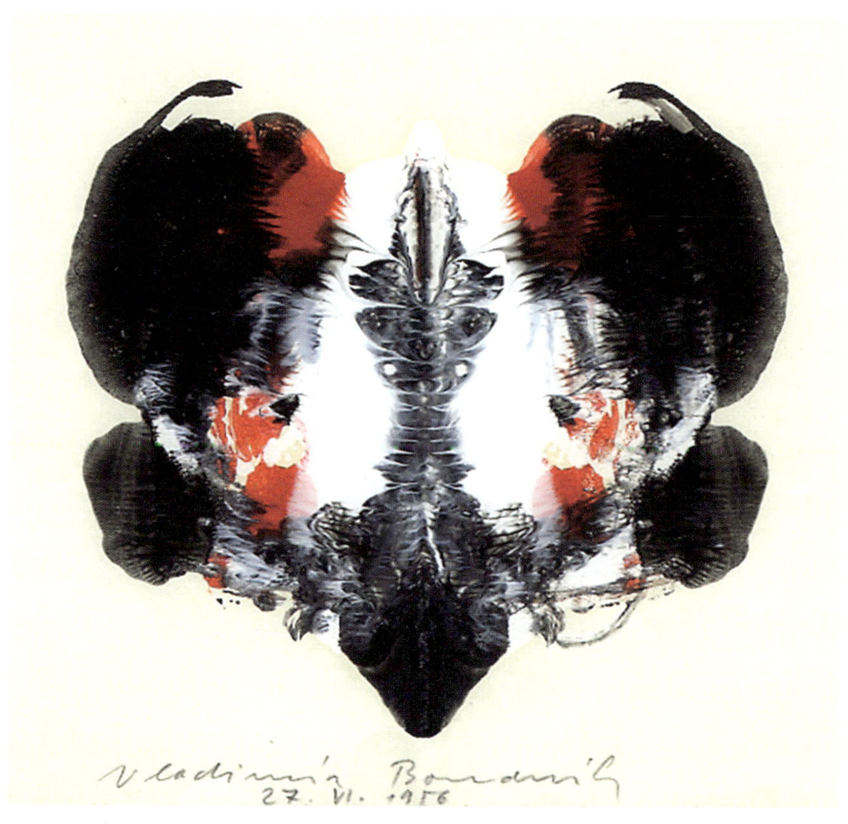

Corpus Delecti, Explosionalist Editions, car paint on paper, 1956

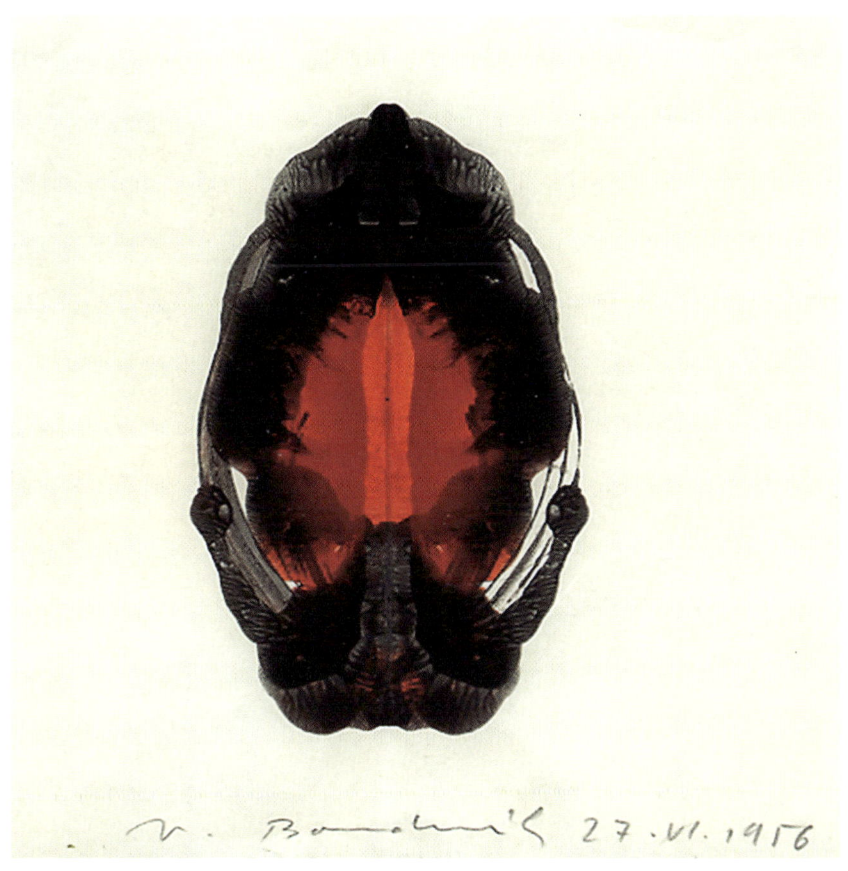

Corpus Delecti, Explosionalist Editions, car paint on paper, 1956

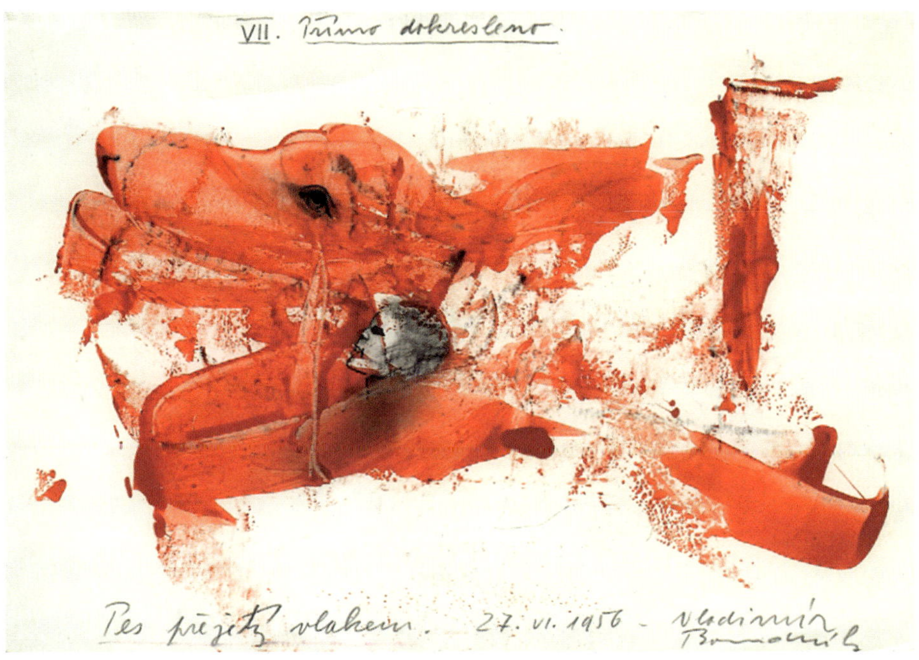

Corpus Delecti, "Dog run over by a train," Explosionalist Editions, car paint & pencil on paper, 1956

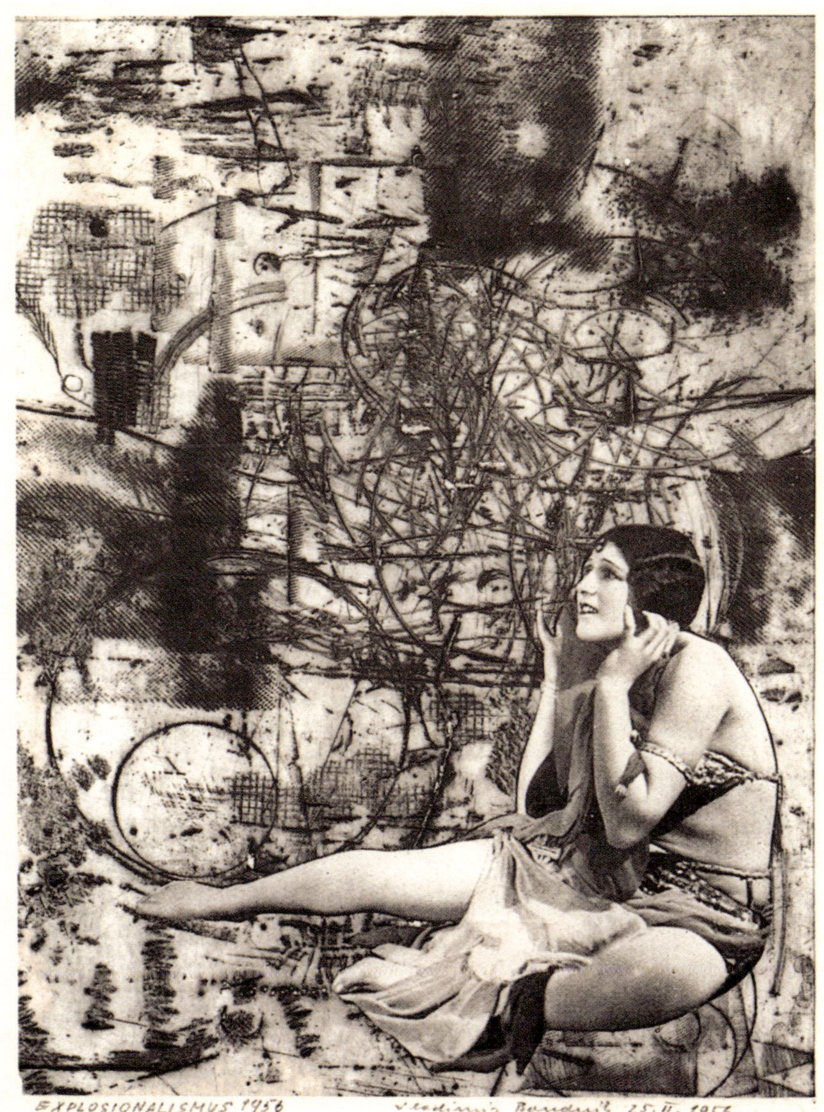

Explosionalism, active print & collage, 1956

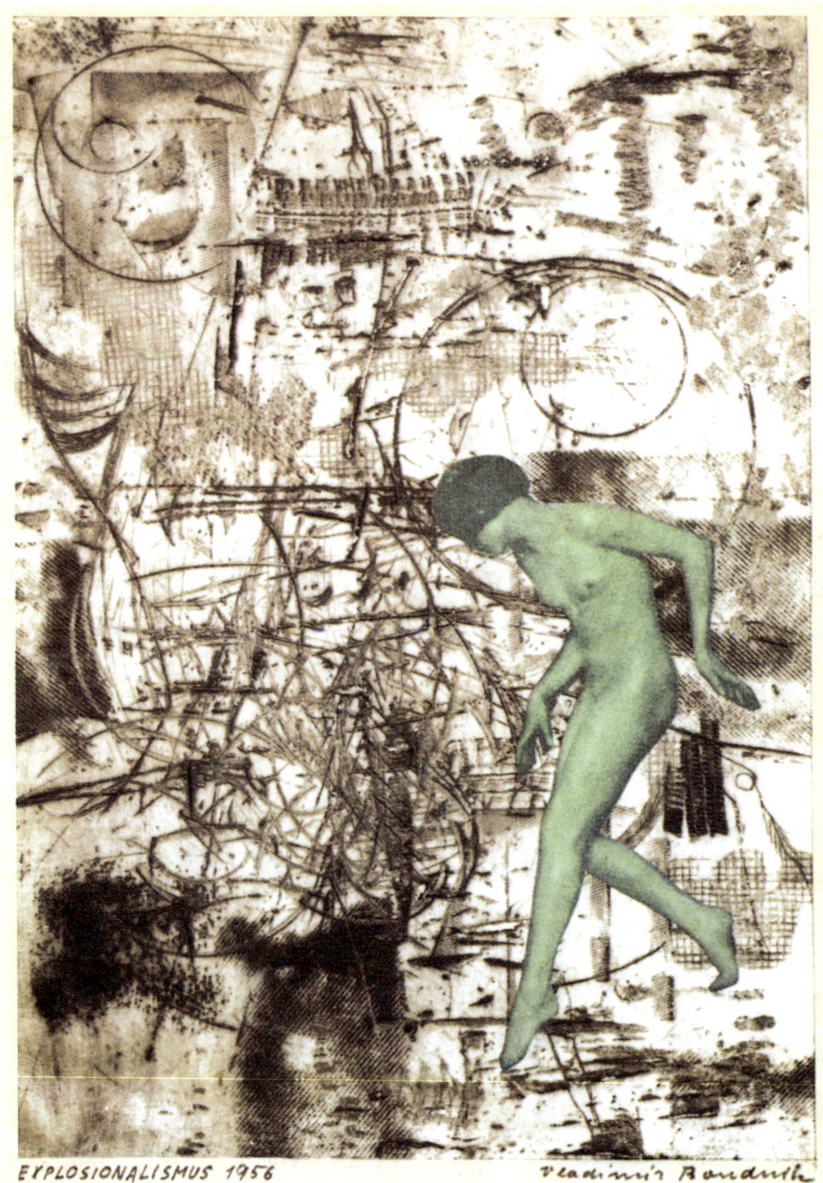

Explosionalism, active print & collage, 1956

EPILOGUE, OR ABDICATION

This tract was read almost twenty-three years ago in Libeň, at 24 The Levee of Eternity Street. It was delivered by a young man in the company of other young folk, some of whom had already started on their path while others were just at the beginning. To a person these youth passionately wanted to work, they loved to work, but not just any work, it had to be work that afforded them the freedom to realize their talents. They had arrived at a crossroads, and they clasped hands for each to follow the direction in which they felt called. This text was lost and forgotten, then rediscovered, and it's interesting to see how much of it has come to pass, as resolution, as prophecy, or as romantic gibberish. And it's interesting to see that one graphic artist, one painter, one sculptor, one poet-philosopher from this group, working day and night over those twenty-three years, did indeed achieve something of real value. Nearly a quarter of a century from the time they went their separate ways they have become the consciousness of a generation that had seemed lost but was far from it, and they have brought fame to Prague literature and contributed new approaches and methods to the visual arts. Who wrote "Abdication" and who read it out? I cannot say for sure, and it's not important. Maybe it was Egon Bondy, maybe Zbyněk Sekal, maybe Jana Krejcarová, maybe Mikuláš Medek. Besides, the important thing is not the signature but what is universal, anonymous, even if signed . . . Well, I'll leave it to readers to walk behind the flapping pinions of "Abdication" to sweep up from the wings of the text fanning them as many feathers as needed to stuff their pillows and cushions . . .

Autumn, 1973

All that remains is for us to say what it is we want. Everything else has already happened. We need to state what we want to do, how we want to live, how we want to think. What we want to love.

All ideologies, all worldviews, are distinguished without exception by their intolerance. All are formulated by a particular segment of society either for itself alone or for another group, but all claim validity for all people. You only need to look around yourself, you only need to look back into the distant and recent past.

We are aware that we, too, belong to a certain social stratum. Up to now our station was as follows: We belonged to the bourgeoisie. Within the bourgeoisie we belonged to the petite bourgeoisie. Within the petite bourgeoisie we belonged to the intelligentsia. Within the intelligentsia we belonged . . . where exactly did we belong? Where do we belong? We know only this: Our relationship to the means of production is nil, because we do not work and have no intention to. If we ever had such aspirations or were coerced into working, it was without our awareness and against our will. We know the future holds the same, that we will have to work, but even in the future it will be against our will. All that matters is that it not be without our knowledge, that we are damn well aware of it, as in the future we'll be aware of many other things as well.

We still need to state what it is we want. And we must once and for all establish, once and for all articulate, this principle: If we inadvertently create an ideology, from an inner need or out of self-defense, we will never try to persuade ourselves of this ideology's applicability to anyone who isn't one of us. It is better not to dwell on any commonalities, they will always exist. We don't want allies, we are self-reliant because we have to be. Everything else is just an illusion, and therefore a lie. Yet we don't seek to completely shun the society we live in, we don't want to shut our eyes to the society around us. This would mean death, and our love of life is so strong it's difficult for others to comprehend.

It would be good to understand how we've reached this point, what came before us, and what path we've taken up till now. And also, and it's no peripheral matter, if our consciences are clear.

What is certain is that we were preceded by others who were similar to what we've been and who we are now. As the historical situation was different, they were different people, but even they rejected the same things we reject, or at least similar things. After all, it's their example that to some extent has shown us what to do. The difference, at least the principal difference, is that their hopes were of a completely different order than are our hopes today. They hoped the proletarian revolution would put an end to hardship and eradicate everything they found stifling and disdained, that it would finally be possible to breathe and to live as each wanted. Some of them have recently come to the sad realization that this isn't the case. Their mistake, however, is in generalizing this realization, of elevating it to their ideology, or better said, broadening it into an ideology for all by turning their disappointment and their catastrophe into disappointment and catastrophe for everyone, or they at least try to convince others of this. They are mistaken.

We do not believe the proletarian revolution has changed or is changing only very little. (To be clear, we contend that the capitalist order is condemned to the dustbin of history, and we take solace in this fact. At least something would be happening.) We know that, on the contrary, the changes taking place or that will take place are in reality more monumental than any previous revolutionary change. The error made by these desperate souls, who otherwise deserve our admiration and respect and whom we've replaced, has been to confuse their hopes and disillusionment with the hopes and disillusionment of others, thereby finding themselves, through their own fault, on the other side in such isolation that they have an increasingly woolly and distorted view of the world around them. And though we reject acolytes and acclaim from any quarter, our objectivity remains unclouded. The point is this: The majority of those who've suddenly found themselves in this social order are no more miserable than before, and are, and will be, even happier and more satisfied.

What would be the point of foisting our dissent, our disillusion, our disgust on any of them? We would be impeding their happiness. We would be introducing confusion into their otherwise perfectly ordered lives, which finds fulfillment in work. And nothing would be achieved by it. Being accursed is out the question for us. Apart from the futility of asserting our ideas, it's actually inconceivable that the number of those espousing ideas intrinsic to us and to a few apprehensive onlookers could increase to any appreciable degree.

And our hopes? They were tremendous, and therefore our disillusionment was, too. It's now behind us, but it does no harm to briefly recapitulate.

At the time the lives of those our age were being decided for them, and also our lives, we were children, or had recently been children. All the things that bothered our peers were for us much more brainless, fatuous, brutal and at the same time more ostentatious. So our defiance was all the more fierce, more unconditional, but . . . also more ostentatious. We couldn't know how it would all turn out. Consequently, through an error in judgment, a lapse, or however you want to call it, we joined our hopes to the hopes of others (we still didn't know one another, nor did we know there were more of us) despite the absence of any affinity whatsoever. Such is always the case.

But why go poking our nose into this, it's not something we'll ever forget, so best to mention it as little as possible. And yet we can't help ourselves. What was it like at that time?

Well, we believed everything then, we knew everything, we understood everything, anything was possible. Our hopes!

In contempt or pity we have turned our backs on those who only want to somehow adapt and either prostitute themselves, hoping for admiration or respect, although getting either is increasingly unlikely, or have inflated their already appallingly ample conceit to such absurd dimensions that they consider it imperative and an exceptional boon to others to continually issue communiqués on the state of their exceedingly interesting and extraordinary natures, their souls, or bulletins on their sordid dalliances. We have never been like them, and if there were ever a danger we were beginning to be like them, we would put a stop to it, at once. They were looking for a way out? Well, in that case, happy trails!

Were mistakes made? Were we duped, were promises made with no intention of being kept? Not at all! The mistake was in us. All in all everything is okay. We shouldn't allow ourselves to be flummoxed by some discrepancies that until now have concealed the true state of affairs. Everything that binds this order to the past is merely indicative of a transitional stage, purely to facilitate a truly epochal transformation from a people forced to work to a people voluntarily working. The entire anachronistic arsenal borrowed from bourgeois democrats and employed by the ideologues of today is nothing more than sweetener to make it easier to take the medicine that will usher the masses into the promised land, and not just illusorily but in actuality, in actuality! All phenomena characteristic of the NEP period or the building of socialism, which is one and the same, are provisional. From this perspective, then, everything really is okay. And our dissent is directed more at what will come than at what is, and again, not for all, but just for we few. To be clear: We never belonged to the previous system. And please . . . we don't belong to the coming one either. This is our lot, difficult at first, and for some of us dangerous, a fate that might easily lead to resignation, self-delusion, and compromise, but a fate that also signifies our hopes, our future, and ultimately, taken to its logical end, the immortality of our kind. We were already aware of this but had yet to draw any conclusions.

Resignation: this implies escape, evasion, an inane construct, but it also means death. And we're so in love with life, so want to live, that our love of life is practically choking us.

Yet we place no hope in this: There will always be people who for a certain time, or always, realize they have nothing in common with others. Namely: It will be difficult at first for them to reconcile with the reality that their entire lives will have to be lived like others and they will have to work until the end of their days. While this means we aren't slated for extinction, that's about all we can expect. Those who come after us will have to deal with it, and, all things considered, they will be different from us. This isn't our concern, nor is it our hope. After all, we'll end up being the object of their ridicule and tears, because their sorrows and their hopes will be greater than ours.

Is reality so risible to us? Do we view it with irony? Are we suited to the role of supercilious critics? Not in the least. For this reason the terms that until recently were meant to pigeonhole us and define our relationship to reality smack of spitefulness and irony, and as such are imprecise, even though there is much truth in them if these terms are understood primarily as part of an agenda. We are, then, at the beginning of the journey. It is incumbent that we start on it as soon as possible and stick to it, that we do so deliberately, that we are prepared, otherwise it will be too late. So this is our ideology, our worldview, if you will. It is absolutely necessary that we look reality square in the face, only among us is this truly possible. We must strive for maximum awareness of everything around us, we must record everything as accurately as possible, understand all things in their true contexts. Though difficult at first, the time has come for us to begin and be done with this craven vacillation, this sitting on the fence, this looking over our shoulders, this regurgitating a litany of protests, which are completely useless and have long been devoid of any authenticity. Moreover, no one outside of ourselves can be counted on to agree with us. It's not that others don't matter, they matter only to themselves alone, yet they are useful to us as material who gladly subject themselves daily to the loveliest autopsy under our steady fingers. Vivisection. It depends on each one of us the extent to which we jettison what we have in common with others. Let no one entertain the idea, even in your dreams, to found a new Church. Only the communists have managed this, and they had favorable preconditions rooted in the nature of their cause. We would be unscathed, but any one of us who seriously attempted to do this would be crushed. And such a person would certainly have to lie a great deal, either to himself or to others, or to both at once.

We want to follow our own path, which is still virtually unknown to us. We don't want to resemble others, whose faces look more and more like the faces of morons. In any case, this judgment means little as they also take us for morons. That's the way it's always been. We don't want their forms of happiness. Whoever of us will find continuing on this path too arduous, all is not lost. The radiant socialist future will be open to you.

The door is wide open.

EXPLOSIONALIST TEXTS

by Uladimír Boudník

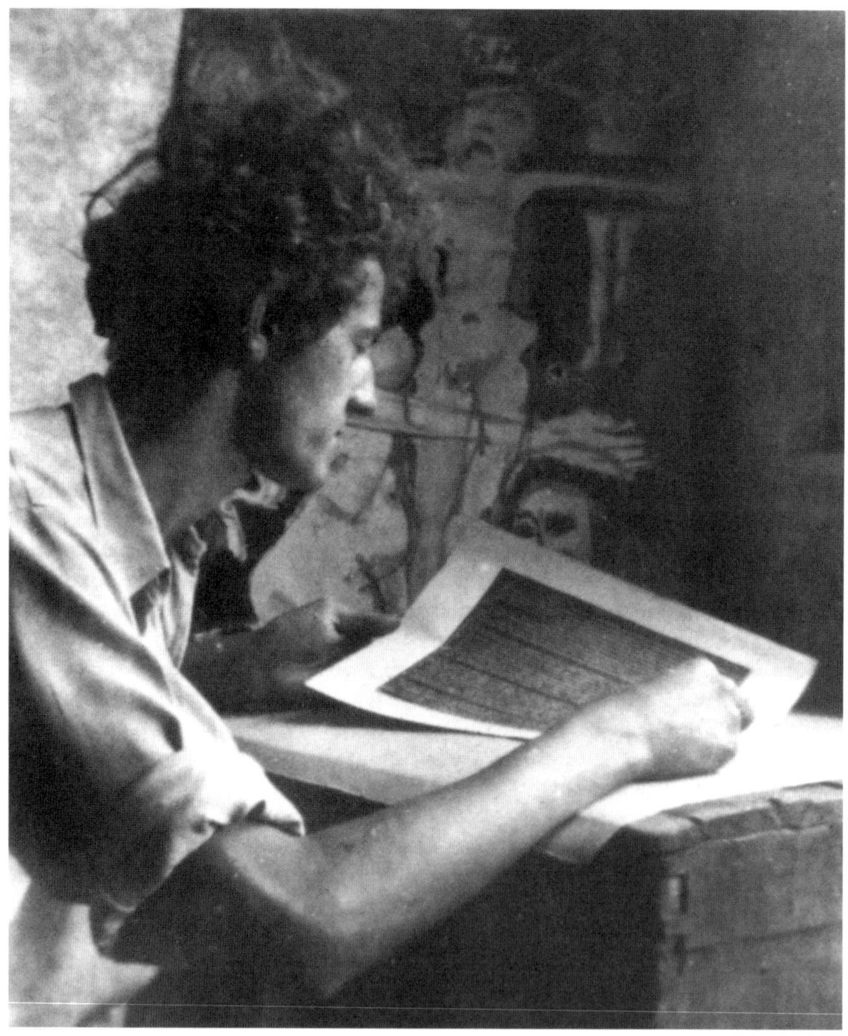

Vladimír Boudník with a print of Manifesto of Explosionlism No. 1, drypoint on three individual plates, 1949

MANIFESTO NO. 1 : ART — EXPLOSIONALISM

March 24, 1949, Prague

People! You penetrate the mysteries of science, society, your very selves. Yet some aspects of the world weigh on you. It is art and its mouthpieces. How many of you have stood, often completely befuddled, before the paintings of certain artists and walked away in frustration and regret at your incomprehension. The numerous films and hundreds of promotional texts that have appeared have largely done nothing to deepen your interest in the subject. My hope is that after reading these lines not only will your interest be awakened but many of you will be better artists than those who have previously disheartened you. Greater, if your life is lived more fully than the lives of these said artists. Picasso, Surrealists, the gaggle of modernists, all will be comprehensible to you. The aureole of divinity will fall from their heads. The world will tremble before the advent of an art erupting from the people. Our planet will be an abundant treasure trove of forms and new inspirations, ushering in the artistic apex of humankind.

Analysis: Every so often you randomly make the acquaintance of a stranger, and then you no longer see each other and ten years pass without a thought of him. You meet again a decade later, and at that moment you realize you've seen this person somewhere before. The shape of his face prompts in you a memory based on images formed in the past. The feelings and experiences stored in your brain operate in exactly the same way, and even if only stored in the unconscious they constitute you as the final outcome in a chain of successive present moments. When you create a picture, its composition derives from prior influences, older or more recent, that is, inspiration is its basis. With respect to the course of the cosmos, no one, therefore, can preempt the present — except with respect to the actions of one's contemporaries.

Everyone remembers using "fantasy" at times to conceive from clouds, rock faces, molten lead at Christmastime . . . a variety of mundane shapes. The exact same process is at work when you look at a flaking wall or marble. In the blotches you see faces, figures, surfaces become space, everything blends together, is animated. Mental images are actually triggered here by the accretion of surface shapes corresponding to your visions. What you actually see is your own life converted into two dimensions — that is, into a surface. The train of imagination is able to construct from basic elements hundreds upon hundreds of original forms and configurations. Understand: it is grounded in life experiences and the cognizance of them evoked by blotches. Some of you attend school to learn how to draw and paint. After five or six years you've accomplished what you set out to do, and more often than not that's the end of it. Many times the flame of enthusiasm goes out during these years of study, and despite the craftsmanship you display, you have nothing to say to the world. Yet if you were to focus on creating work with the help of blots, you would learn how to express yourself visually in a matter of days, a few weeks at most. And how much richer your work would be. Even richer the more you experience in adult life as compared to those academy trained artists. And it makes no difference if you're a miner, chemical engineer, housewife . . . , was not the world of culture enriched the most by persons engaged in life? Naturally art schools will continue to exist, but unlike in the past, they will no longer teach the craft of art and will produce instead art from their collective.

If from the time we're born we had lived in a white room, seeing nothing other than the white walls, our imagination would be nil. We, however, daily see thousands of forms, thousands of movements. All of these are stored in the "spirals" of our brain even if at times subconsciously. If circumstances awaken in you a strong enough interest to express yourself, then expressing this inner state should be embraced. Blotches will facilitate the actualization of your desire. Your soul will be rid of preconceptions about art through overcoming them and above all through comprehending a new art. To repeat: The artist, that is, anyone who honestly wishes to express their interiority, must proceed from the realism of life. And life today is so profuse that it would be a sin and transgression against present and future generations to let feelings and knowledge die alongside humanity for no other reason than its inability to give of itself. Look around you! At the grimy wall, marble, wood grain . . . , what you see is your interiority. Don't underrate blotches, trace them with a finger, trace them on paper . . . empower your inner mind. Why continue to be swayed by foreign gurus and grovel as an epigone at their feet? Create your own inspirations. You have something to say to the world! I believe that new geniuses will arise from your ranks. Geniuses of a healthy life.

Those of a conservative bent will claim that creating art "from" blots is governed by chance. Yet I maintain that this method entails more consistency, sensibility, and artistic discipline than a method that actualizes mental images through mannerism, commonplace sketching, or even by using photographs roughly corresponding to one's visions. In these latter instances a work is produced that is often completely alien to the original idea. The painting should never be a snapshot. We have photography for this. The painting must be a "filmstrip" chock-full of suspense and psychological explosions concentrated on an immobile surface shown in an infinitely short time. The movement of the "filmstrip" is replaced here by the movement of the viewer's imagination and fantasy. I am aware that many artists are inspired by blots . . . But in that case, why have they been lauded as "geniuses of divine imagination"?

v PRAZE DNE 15. DUBNA 1949   ČECHY.

LIDÉ. STOJÍME TĚSNĚ PŘED ATOMOVOU DOBOU. DESETITISÍCE TOVÁREN S DESETIMILIONOVOU ARMÁDOU PRACOV-
NÍKŮ EXPERIMENTUJE, BUDUJE A SNAŽÍ SE OBOHATIT NAŠI PLANETU O DALŠÍ POZNATKY. ČINNOST MINULÝCH
STALETÍ, SE SVÝMI PODNĚTY, JE V HRUBÝCH RYSECH SKONČENA A VĚDOMOSTI O NÍ ULOŽENY V KNIHÁCH,
PŘÍSTUPNÝCH NEJŠIRŠÍ VEŘEJNOSTI. Z TOHO DŮVODU PRACOVNÍK S KRUMPÁČEM MÁ PRÁVO MÍTI TENTÝŽ PO-
CIT DŮLEŽITOSTI, JAKO ČLOVĚK, RÝSUJÍCÍ SOUČÁST STROJE. DNES KAŽDÝ GRAMOTNÝ JEDINEC, PŘI TROCHU
SOUSTŘEDĚNOSTI, NAČERPÁ ZNALOSTI, KTERÉ PŘED NĚKOLIKA DESETILETÍMI DĚLALI Z JEJICH MAJITELE VĚDCE.
CELÝ SVĚT JE NABIT SNAHOU PO NOVÉM TVŮRČÍM POHYBU! — A JAK SE K TÉMTO ZMĚNÁM STAVÍ UMĚLCI?
VYPADÁ TO, JAKO BY JEJICH ŘADY PŘEVÁŽNĚ TVOŘILI NEMOHOUCÍ, VYŽÍVAJÍCÍ SE KONSERVATIVNÍ FANATICI.
SKUPINA „NADREALISTŮ" KDYSI PONĚKUD VYHOVOVALA SOUČASNOSTI, KDYBY JEJICH NASTUPCI, DYCHTÍCÍ PO
TAJUPLNÉ BOHAROVNOSTI, CELÉ SNAŽENÍ NEZVRHLI A NEODSOUDILI UMĚLECKÝ SMĚR DO ÚLOHY KRESLIČE TA-
JENEK V DĚTSKÝCH ČASOPISECH. DNEŠNÍMU USPOŘÁDÁNÍ SVĚTA ODPOVÍDÁ JEDINĚ EXPLOSIONALIS-
MUS. SMĚR, KTERÝ POVÝŠÍ KAŽDÉHO ČLENA KOLEKTIVA NA ABSOLUTNĚ VŠEMOHOUCÍHO ČLOVĚKA, NE-
BOŤ JEHO VÝBOJ PŮJDE NA ÚKOR VESMÍRU A NIKOLI NA ÚKOR BLIŽNÍHO. MOZEK EXPLOSIONALISTY BUDE
NACHÁZETI NAPLNĚNÍ VE ZMNOŽOVÁNÍ TVARŮ A DUŠEVNÍCH HODNOT, V TRILIONECH A TRILIONECH
KUBÍKŮ VESMÍRNÉHO PROSTORU. KAŽDÝ Z VÁS BUDE UMĚLCEM, ZBAVÍLI SE PŘEDSUDKŮ A NETEČNOSTI.
ANALYSA + SYNTHESA: VĚTŠINA Z VÁS SI ZA POMOCI FANTASIE VYTVÁŘÍ Z MRAKŮ, SKAL, NEBO Z
OLOVA LITÉHO O VÁNOCÍCH, RŮZNÉ SVĚTSKÉ PODOBY. PRÁVĚ TAK JE TOMU, ZAHLEDÍTELI SE NA OPRÝS-
KANOU ZEĎ, NEBO ŽÍLY MRAMORU. VIDÍTE TVÁŘE, POSTAVY··· VŠE SE PROLÍNÁ, OŽIVUJE. UVEDENÉ
PRVKY ROZJITŘILY STARÉ PROŽITKY, ULOŽENÉ VE VAŠEM MOZKU, VE FORMĚ VZPOMÍNEK. VY VIDÍTE SVOJE
NITRO PŘEVEDENÉ DO DVOU ROZMĚRŮ; TEDY DO PLOCHY. STAČÍ PŘEKRESLITI, NEBO PŘEMALOVATI VIDĚNÉ NA PA-
PÍR. ZMOCŇUJETE SE SVÉHO NITRA A TÍM JE AUTOMATICKY ČINÍTE SROZUMITELNÉ ŠIROKÉ VEŘEJNOSTI.
JEDEN A TÝŽ SHLUK SKVRN BUDE STO LIDEM PŘIPOMÍNATI STO RŮZNÝCH PODOB A KOMBINACÍ. VIDINY SE
ŘÍDÍ PODLE STUPNĚ NÁLADY A NA ZÁKLADĚ ŽIVOTNÍCH PROŽITKŮ POZOROVATELE. JE LOGICKÉ, ŽE NEVIDĚL-LI
ČLOVĚK NĚJAKÝ EXOTICKÝ KVĚT NEBO SOUČÁST STROJE, NEUMÍ ANI JEDNO ANI DRUHÉ NAKRESLIT; A PAKLI
UVEDENÉ VĚCI VYPLYNOU MU ZE SKVRN, ZDAJÍ SE MU NEPOCHOPITELNÉ, AČ PRO DRUHÉHO JSOU JASNÉ.
PŘED SKVRNY MŮŽETE, POD VLIVEM INSPIRACE PŘISTOUPIT SE ZÁMĚREM. MNOHÉ Z OBRAZŮ, KTERÉ VÁS U-
TVRZOVALY O GENIALITĚ JEJICH TVŮRCE, BYLY VYTVOŘENY NA UVEDENÝCH ZÁKLADECH. JE-LI VÁŠ ŽIVOT PRO-
ŽITÝ BOHATŠÍM ZPŮSOBEM NEŽLI ŽIVOT VÝTVARNÍKA, KTERÝ VÁS DŘÍVE DEPRIMOVAL, BUDE TÉŽ BOHATŠÍ VÁŠ
UMĚLECKÝ PROJEV. JSTE-LI MANUELNÍ PRACOVNÍK TAK SE NEVYMLOUVEJTE ŽE SE VÁM CHVĚJE RUKA. UMĚ-
NÍ DNEŠKA VYŽADUJE ŽIVOTNÍ PRAVDU A NE POVRCHNÍ, ŠKOLNĚ NAUČENOU ŽONGLÉRSKOU ELEGANCI!
OBRAZ NESMÍ BÝT MOMENTKOU. K TOMU ÚČELU SLOUŽÍ FOTOGRAFIE. OBRAZ MUSÍ BÝTI „FILMOVÝM PÁSEM
O NESČÍSLNÉM MNOŽSTVÍ NAPĚTÍ A PSYCHOLOGICKÝCH EXPLOSÍ ZHUŠTĚNÝCH DO NEHYBNÉ PLOCHY A
PŘEDVEDENÝCH V NEKONEČNĚ KRÁTKÉM ČASE, ZA SOUČINNOSTI DIVÁKOVY POHYBOVÉ FANTASIE-

Manifesto of Explosionlism No. 2, lithograph, 1949

MANIFESTO OF EXPLOSIONALISM NO. 2

In Prague, April 15, 1949, Bohemia

People. We stand on the cusp of the atomic age. Tens of thousands of factories with tens of millions of military personnel are experimenting, constructing, and endeavoring to enrich our planet with more knowledge. The activity of past centuries, with its stimuli, has generally run its course and the knowledge of it deposited in books available to the general public. For this reason, a laborer with a pickaxe has a right to feel as important as the designer of a machine component. Today each and every literate individual with just a little concentration can absorb knowledge that just a few short decades ago would've made savants of those who possessed it. The pursuit of new creative movement galvanizes the entire world! — And how are artists reacting to these changes? It appears their ranks are predominantly filled by impotent, self-indulgent, parochial fanatics. The group of "Surrealists" had to an extent made their concessions to the present day, yet their successors, craving an arcane eminence, subverted all their efforts and consigned their art movement to the drawing of word puzzles for children's magazines. Only EXPLOSIONALISM responds to the present world order. It is a movement that elevates each member of the collective to absolute omnipotence, as their detonation comes at the expense of the universe and not to the detriment of their fellow humans. The Explosionalist intellect will find fulfillment in the proliferation of forms and psychic values, in the trillions and trillions of cubic meters of cosmic space. Each of you will become an artist if you rid yourselves of preconceptions and apathy.

ANALYSIS + SYNTHESIS: Most of you use imagination to conceive a variety of mundane shapes from clouds, rock faces, or molten lead at Christmastime. The exact same process is at work when you look at a flaking wall or marble veining. You see faces, figures . . . everything blends together, is animated. These said elements have triggered old experiences, stored in your brain in the form of memories. You see your interiority converted into two dimensions, into a surface. You only need to redraw or repaint these visions on paper. You take possession of your inner mind and thereby automatically make it intelligible for society at large. One and the same cluster of blots will remind a hundred people of a hundred different shapes and combinations. Visions are governed by the observer's state of mind and life experiences. It stands to reason that if someone has never seen an exotic flower or a machine part, then he will not know how to draw either one; and if these images emerge from blots, then they will seem incomprehensible to him while being intelligible to another. Under the sway of inspiration, you can approach blots with a sense of purpose. Many of the paintings that have convinced you of the artist's genius were created on this basis. If your life is fuller than the lives of artists who have previously disheartened you, then your artistic expression will also be fuller. If you are a manual laborer, don't use your shaky hand as an excuse. The art of today requires life truths and not the superficial acrobatic flair taught in art school!

The painting should never be a snapshot. Photography serves this purpose. The painting must be a "filmstrip" chock-full of suspense and psychological explosions concentrated on an immobile surface and shown in an infinitely short time in synergy with the viewer's kinetic imagination.

EXPLOSIONALISM : PREFACE TO A LETTER

March 21, 1950

In March 1949, we published for the first time a brief summary of our thoughts on art under the heading EXPLOSIONALISM.

Because circumstances had insulated us from the conclusions drawn by others on art trends, we were not swept into the vortex of fashionable leftist epigonism and were free to experience those slices of intellectual disciplines we might have otherwise considered a waste of time.

Having established that the human is a cosmic form with the ability to convert "minimal" impulses into "maximal" results, we see that disinterest in the visual arts consists in an inability to perceive said minimal impulses.

EXPLOSIONALISTS did not endeavor to create, in conjunction with all available impulses, a narrowly defined art movement but instead to legitimize, from the human scientific point of view, elements having validity for the visual arts until such time as the human organism undergoes significant modification.

We truly became aware of Surrealist techniques and their use of decalcomania only a few months (July 1949) after we issued our first manifesto.

Our earlier mistaken conviction that we were the only ones interested in legitimizing creative work, particularly work arising from a train of free associations, was the chief reason why we sought support for our views in discussions with others.

EXPLOSIONALISM is an aggregation of ever-evolving principles and insights.

For these reasons, only the quintessence of these principles and insights is discussed below.

Over the course of the past year we have often put ourselves in the shoes of those who've prejudicially decried our activity as wholly dubious or showed indifference to it. We completely understand them. For someone on the way to the swimming pool or a dance, for those with their "own" concerns, or for those who are actually artists or aspiring to be — then it's "no wonder" their brains are not stimulated to take an interest in the problems of another or to write a single reply to a multipage letter.

SUMMARY OF EXPLOSIONALISM'S CENTRAL VIEWS AND TENETS
ON ART UP TO 1950

The cosmos at present is an outcome of the inertia of a prime mover, eternally distant in the past. "Prime mover" can be lumped in with ideas represented by the concept of COMPLIANT THINKING. Compliant thinking is characteristic of the human mind searching for the correct response to the introduction of millions upon trillions of miscellaneous ideas without arriving at a satisfactory answer. For example: Someone inquiring about the end of the universe, the origin of the cosmos, etc. (Compliant thinking is often eliminated from human consciousness through a provisionally plausible explanation or by a loss of stimuli to take an interest. The most well-known escape is superstition. Many people cope with compliant thinking in a period when it is supplemented in a different milieu by conclusive science-based knowledge. — Mathematics, chemistry . . .) (The last lines are more a variation of compliant thinking . . .)

Due to space limitations, I will not discuss the concepts of reason, emotion, cognition, the unconscious, "intuition," dream and a hundred others, at most they will be alluded to . . .

Will is a brain activity sparked by stimuli, at least one of which guides the synchronous work of body and mind until such time as a goal is achieved. (Or until the activity proves to be futile.) Many times the form of stimuli changes during the process of consummating an intention, but the energy of the replaced stimuli is still contained within. For those who were not able to follow our beginnings, I'll mention here the essential aspects of our views from March 1949 . . . The world will tremble before the advent of art. Our planet will be an abundant treasure trove of forms and new inspirations. It will usher in the artistic apex of humankind . . .

Analysis: Every so often you make the acquaintance of a stranger. Then you no longer see each other and many years pass without remembering you met him. When you meet again, the shape of his face — if nothing has fundamentally changed — prompts in you a memory based on images formed in the past. The feelings and other experiences stored in your brain organ, "body," operate in exactly the same way, and even if only stored in the unconscious they constitute you as the final outcome in a sequence of successive present moments. When you create a picture, its composition derives from prior influences, whether older or more immediate. — Knowledge informs us that with respect to the course of the cosmos no one can preempt the present, except with respect to the actions of one's contemporaries. — Everyone remembers having used "fantasy" to conceive from clouds, rock faces, molten lead at Christmastime . . . a variety of mundane shapes. The exact same process is at work when you look at a dilapidated wall or slab of marble. In the blotches you see faces, figures, things; everything blends together, is animated! Mental images are actually triggered here by the accretion of analogous forms you've encountered in your life. You replace the third dimension — from the haptic point of view — with an inner vision, therefore, a fourth dimension . . . The painting must be a "filmstrip" chock-full of suspense and psychological explosions concentrated on an immobile surface and shown in an infinitely short time. The movement of the "filmstrip" is replaced here by the viewer's kinetic imagination . . .

This recapitulation comes off as relatively primitive, but with the distance of one year we see that its content was such a powerful provocation that we were able to wrest human senses from the centuries-old mire of sterile biases and liberate humanity's creative potency in a way commensurate with our technologically advanced age. We believe Explosionalism will be the current kindling the art of our planet!

If someone wanted to learn the form of a thing in the most absolute way possible, or at least its exterior, then it would need to be observed from millions of angles, in other words, from the spherical space enveloping the given object . . .

Each human *expression,* inasmuch as it's the outcome of *many impulses,* the final form of which is the very state of the person in the midst of expression, is *subjective.* Locating and determining objectivity or subjectivity can only be attempted on the impulses. Only here might we indicate if an impulse is objective, arising from social influences, or subjective, arising in effect from the anatomical makeup of the figure under scrutiny. Ostensible objectivity is attributed to an individual, therefore, because his expression is channeled by influences that have a consonant effect on his fellowman, lending him the veneer of a person expressing himself objectively. (For example, during an earthquake, in a region of established convention and the like.)

Many people exhibit an interesting form of epigonism. They adopt some proficiency in drawing from another and then fumble around "bemused," and for no other reason than to assure themselves they are not epigones. If they succeed, it's because old impulses are suppressed in the conscious by impulses and discoveries from the fumbling around period . . . Explosionalism elevates viewers from the "dust" of medieval wonderment to an intellectual level whereby they feel themselves a co-creator brimming with imagination . . .

It is essential to be aware of the elements in art that can be adopted by mechanical progress. (Photography, film, radio . . .) In the present state of the ordinary "world," it's naive to revere paintings only because they were created by hand. Viewers such as these hinder progress. They don't realize that the "psychic" influence of photography and film operates on the nervous system and judgment of the artist, who is conscious of the impact these elements have on the viewer, who subconsciously is compelled to compare the preciseness of photography with the work of art (painting). In this instance, the artist sees the impact of a painting, frequently taking a year to complete, superseded by the photographer's few minutes of effort. This point could be fleshed out further . . .

We have machines, cities, discoveries like at no other time in human history. What prevents us from using this reality to break away from imitation and the dependence on foreign models?! We are in an era when the current revitalizing world culture could easily originate in Prague . . .

With the advances made by the news media, it is in the power of the public to understand the work of art with minimal time lag. It is a primitive prejudice that the latest "tendency" can be understood only after all prior movements have been exhausted. Wrong! Many times the latest "tendency," as is the case with Explosionalism, makes it possible to understand itself as well as all prior movements. (We touched on the quintessential human qualities identical in both primeval and present-day generations in our analysis of the emergence of prehistoric drawings . . .)

If a work of art is enthusiastically accepted by society, then it is absolutely legitimate to defend this work, even if the artist is later condemned as inferior. The verdict is written by those who are unaware that propelled by new inspirations they were rejecting old inspirations as lacking fulfillment, even if amid the interplay of the two the work of art was created, which will give fulfillment to others. If you stand under a burning light bulb and look through the window into the darkness, you will see projected on the border between light and dark the inside of your eye, through which you gaze, in the form of a target the color of night, garlanded with veins. The projection fluctuates in size between one meter and several centimeters. (Subject to the border of darkness . . .)

After reading this through we see that instead of a summary of insights we have again merely produced a compilation of accumulated notes; we hope they prove essential.

The Explosionalists
Prague, March 27, 1950

March 29, 1950

It stands to reason that if you've never seen an exotic flower, for example, then you won't be able to see it in blotches either. And if you see some analogous shape, you won't know what it means.

It's important to realize that film, photography, and the images surrounding us operate on our sight organs and thus create the positive preconditions for the development of Explosionalism.

"Religious visions" originate in the train of associative thought free of compliant thinking. (Afflicted with convention.)

It's madness to exclude humankind from the laws of cosmic evolution . . .

The artist whose work is consciously derived from free association gives the impression of a lunatic to others. Denunciation is the child of rashness.

It's proving necessary to establish principles in art that will give people some footing as progress advances and will lessen the danger of frivolous sentiments deepening the chasm of misunderstanding between the work of art and humanity.

The need to introduce Explosionalism into sculpture, music . . .

TO THE ACADEMY OF APPLIED ARTS [UMPRUM]

February 24, 1951
Prague

Progress exists! As do an endless number of motion vectors. Motion . . . billions of movements ensuing from preceding movements. Many of you gesture with your hands, indicating unhappiness, desperation, enthusiasm.

The older generation doesn't understand the middle generation — their own fault. The older generation doesn't understand that they were once a middle generation. It doesn't understand that it creates and articulates ideas that partly form its environment, and at the same time it doesn't understand the outcomes it has contributed to.

The visual arts flounder in those areas where the viewer is excluded beforehand as a real factor. In the midst of creating, the artist inarguably attains inner fulfillment. It would be a mistake, however, for the artist to reckon with the person/viewer as the final component. The wretch doesn't realize that if the public were left out of the equation the same degree of fulfillment could be attained through creative work, dreaming, or a shiny toy. These "self-sufficient geniuses" rant and rave if someone knowledgeably critiques their work. They say: ". . . we like birdsong and we don't ask why . . ." Naturally they fail to realize that just like certain objects of technology have their peak years and downturns before then being subsumed into other objects, so too this line about birdsong is contingent on events and a network of movements that will allow it to stand out.

The young generation wants to know essence! . . . (birdsong = feeling of safety). "Our consciousness" impacts millions of new values. It's not enough to tackle the essence of a lathe only with regard to its inherent structure. We need to observe how it functions in X Y settings. We need to see it as part of the equation of cosmic evolution. It's pathetic to get into arguments over "if a friend is waiting or not on the other side of the wall" and not take a peek. Maybe you (who are reading this letter) were the ones who attacked us as we were trying to create pictures on the street. You couldn't help but have in mind the spontaneous authenticity of works created by today's acclaimed painters.

You argued: "Paintings can't be offered like an apple." I say: False! Many paintings should be offered more readily than an apple! An apple decays much more slowly than the value of a painting. Have those lives of artists so hoodwinked you by their bitter tone that some of you naturally think you'll only be understood in 100, 200 . . . years? I don't mean to imply you shouldn't be understood until then — just the opposite! You should be part of the world's consciousness for the entirety of this time. Besides, in most cases it's just that the ground is too barren for conscious change that makes possible the "coronation of artworks" during a given era. Judged objectively: Artists live in their time along with their peers. Artists need to be able to stimulate their contemporaries to comprehend their art since the same influences surround them both, albeit the overall impact on their consciousness differs. (Artists should be communicative to counterbalance the convulsive alienation of others . . .) It's logical that the work of art be a specific record, a seismogram as it were, that it be a testimony for future generations to aid in their study and understanding of progress.

Today isn't the time for opaque, imaginative expressions — maybe the inertia (conventional) is agreeable, but feckless. All values need revaluation.

For the Explosionalists
Vladimír Boudník

Vladimír was welcomed as if he were expected. He leaned his satchel against the wall and sat down on a chair by the stove. Yet first he heard Doctor's words:

"Wires, wires everywhere."

Doctor was perceptive. Nothing wrong with deliberately letting a coil of aluminum wire stick out of his pocket. (Too bad Vladimír didn't find a carpenter's pencil at the bottom of his satchel a moment before. A wire with a yellow pencil at its end makes a weaker impression.) Sitting on the chair, Vladimír adjusted the diameter of the loop several times.

"Who have you strangled?" and Doctor momentarily became a child. "Let me see it. I once caught a badger with something like it. I waited by its burrow . . ." and he abruptly jerked his hands to show how.

"Did you write the letter?" asked Bondy.

"I did, any mail come for me?"

"You got a letter," Doctor informed him.

"Vladimír stood up and went into the next room. On the way he asked, "from Dočekal?" . . . nodding . . . (Intriguing envelope, to keep the contents from being damaged . . .) He returned. Talk. Bondy's turn.

"I was just explaining how Hanes Reegen and I met. I've known him since '47." (Bondy got the names confused, he was thinking of Šmerda.)

"Since '46 for me."

"So a little longer."

"I want to hear it, too."

"Ok, so to repeat: . . . I was walking to Mánes for 10 crown meatloaf. I was 17 . . . Unrationed meatloaf, but they served it on three separate plates and I'd ostentatiously wolf it down. Going from one plate to the next gave me a high. So one day I'm just lounging on the patio . . . in the back . . . you know, where you can walk down Žofín Island . . . yep, that place! I was sitting there nonchalantly, my hair was down to here, I had a tie on, one leg crossed over the other, American socks, you know, so they can be seen, size 5 shoe — custom-made suede — I have such small feet. So I'm sitting there like that when suddenly I see two people approaching me. Total proletarians. Shabby — she was so plain, but even so a skirt up to here, hair in a bun, a kind of blouse, but everything plain. I think to myself, 'What the heck do they want? Free tables are everywhere but they're making for mine.'

" 'Excuse me, we have a bet . . .'

"(They're probably going to tell me I'm a slacker, something about a work brigade, I'm already thinking how I'm going to reply.)

" '. . . I say you're a poet and she says . . . a musician.'

"I was at the time . . . 17 . . . 'to tell the truth, I'm more into literature.' "

"Was it Strouhalová?" asked Vladimír.

"Yes, and Šmerda. To go back to the beginning. We lived at Na Slovance . . ."

"Who lived in that 'madhouse'?"

"Yep, it was your typical Surrealist milieu. The attic was divided into two parts. In one lived the custodian and the other half was reserved for old junk. Six of us slept there. It was Šmerda, Strouhalová, me, Sklenařík, Reegen, and one more, *what* was his name? . . . One time Šmerda and Strouhalová left for a work brigade harvesting hops and Eva's parents sent her to stay with relatives somewhere in the countryside (to keep an eye on her), and I was left there alone. When the work brigade finished Šmerda hung around and Líba came back by herself."

"Líba loved a lot of guys platonically," Vladimír chimed in.

"Also me (it was always conversations). I would bawl for a moment, then she . . . Well. When she came back, it went further. I tossed out all the beds and left this big one . . ."

(Vladimír interrupted): "Like in Mníšek. Fishlová and I had something similar. But that was two pushed together. I remember it. You left for Prague and I
slept with her twice – next to one another. She had nothing on. Just a black sweater,
and we didn't do anything either."

"So we sleep together and in the morning we wake up and want to make tea.
We had it at hand, under the bed. We let the water boil and lie back down — just
any old way, entwined. Suddenly the door opens and in walks Šmerda. He just
stands there looking at us, nothing else. I go downstairs to the john — wearing
pajamas. I come back upstairs and the shit's hit the fan. Strouhalka's bawling her
eyes out and Láďa's all steamed and right away says to me: 'Keep your trap shut.
You're just a Trotskyist anyway — and you do me like this.'"

Vladimír unwittingly cut him off: "Eva's a fox. Really pretty. I knew her from
Falkenburk. Raven-haired, like a Gypsy girl."

"Interesting type, the kind that attracts me to this day," Bondy continued, "she
was like a child in some respects while being physically mature . . . such large eyes.
She and I made the rounds of all the establishments, from The Pygmalion to I
don't even know where. All of it without a crown in our pockets and taxis home.
You had to know us then. I was a complete Christ Child. Angelic face. We would
come somewhere, take a seat, and look around like this. Always someone would
come over, 'such children' — yep, drunk every day.

"Once we were sitting in some joint and it was already 1 a.m. and nothing anywhere. We were fed up. Of course a waiter would pour us what we wanted, but
there was nothing. We didn't have any money for a taxi and to huff it all the way
out to Na Slovance?! So we lay down at the top of the steps to the Academy of
Applied Arts, when all of a sudden three guys come walking past: 'What're you
doing here? Come with us.' We got drunk with them and one took us to his place.
He kicked his wife out into the hall to sleep and we snoozed in peace, and in the
morning, like it was a matter of course, the wife made us breakfast and then we
took a taxi home."

Vladimír went to fetch his satchel and looked in it for a letter he wrote at

U Fleků to H. Todt after a session with Bondy and repeated goodbyes. "I'll read it to you," he began, "is that OK?" he stumbled through it for a moment, "should I continue? it's not boring you?"

"NO, just read!" Doctor assured him.

Near the end Vladimír couldn't read "herein" as it kept coming out as "peer in" since he mistakenly had written over the word at the beginning.

"Give it here." And with Doctor's help it came out correctly as "herein."

"This is the kind of letter I send. Haha!"

Hands in his pockets, Bondy: "Typical, hehe. Typical. Paranoiac masochism."

Vladimír didn't know what these words meant. In addition Doctor jumped in and pointed to the influence of James Joyce. Vladimír gushed: "Yes, I've read the confessions! But I can bring you dated diary notes that show what I've expressed in this letter I'd recorded as purely personal experience way before I read his book. It's a long…"

Bondy, Vladimír, Doctor — a vortex of words.

"Listen, Vladimír," and in that letter, "I admit that if it were," and in that letter, "not for that book I wouldn't have," and in that letter, "written it, but it wouldn't have been any oth," and in that letter … and, "er thing. For example, lamppost. For the most part, I've also read his ideas elsewhere. I've already found 75% of his opin," and in that letter, "ions in books. For Christ's sake, *Vladimír,* and still I've read maybe a tenth of his writing."

Doctor was standing, elbow leaning on the brass headboard of the bed: "And in that letter — — —"

Vladimír got up. He had to walk around the room to keep from puking. He'd been drinking dark beer and was now on the hard stuff . . . Doctor became defensive:

"But 25% is mine." Vladimír acknowledged the poetic quality of Doctor's and Bondy's work. Erben got worked into the discussion. Chaos!

"You shit on folks and someone has to create a connection between them and the work." "We couldn't give a fuck about these folks of yours. Look here, Vladimír!

Your deal is painting, poetry, but for the love of God, stay away from theory."

"And at this very moment, today, when no one gives two shits, there is an opportunity to evaluate everything from new artistic perspectives."

"You, Vladimír, are an arrant idealist," Bondy shouted.

"I'm a materialist."

"STOP!!!" Bondy held his head as he backed up past the stove toward the wall . . . Exchanging places, Bondy was now sitting at the front of the room by the stove.

"I don't identify Explosionalism with Total Realism. You're an unconscious epigone of Surrealism!"

"Not for a long time," Bondy roared, "not for a long time. We left it. Yep, back in '49 . . ."

"You have an inner dependence on Surrealism. All of you look for pure contrast to set yourselves apart. You're wimps because by repudiating Surrealism you lost the impetus to do anything. You've nothing to hold onto. Explosionalism is a brick. You have to reckon with it. Explosionalists are realists . . ."

"Vladimír . . . Let's go take a leak — I've tested this out."

Doctor would rather piss in the sink. The Total Realist and the Explosionalist momentarily parted ways.

"Come here, Vladimír. Would it be possible to get something to drink somewhere? If you add fifty to these two hundred crowns we could go out for something."

Mysterious movements. Vladimír grabbed his sports coat and a pitcher. The pitcher still held 1/4 liter of beer. In the courtyard, over the drainage ditch, he drank it. "Save some for me."

"Here you go. I just had to wet my whistle." "I'll also wet my whistle . . . lead me."

"Shh!" "I'll be quiet." "I'm leaving it unlocked . . . We'll talk outside."

"Vladimír! Look here, I want to see the street as it truly is, realistically, not some blotches onto which one's fantasies are projected!"

"Surely you admit, Zbyněk (leaning in confidentially), that if I'm set on being meticulously scientific, then naturally I'm trying to understand things factually."

"Hold on . . . this is essential. I have a feeling I'm a little light. I left the money at home."

"Quiet, don't bump into anything, there's a banister . . ." "OK . . . I forgot about it."

"Put your hand on it, careful, stairs. This way . . ."

Vladimír and Bondy went to the pub. The publican's wife was there.

"Good evening. Do you have rum? How much for 1/2 liter?"

"300 crowns here."

"Here's 200, how much do you have?"

"80."

Bondy tried to get 1/2 liter. The lady publican refused his identity card for credit. This comes to 270 crowns. The customer gets 8 crowns back.

"Not even a jigger?"

The publican was adamant. Zbyněk's whiskers tickled her neck as he attempted to smuggle his request into her brain. Futile.

When they returned they found Doctor lying in bed, but he got up immediately and drank rum from the blue pitcher and filled up mugs.

The night ended at 4 a.m. with an impromptu brawl between Bondy and Vladimír. That the neighbors ran out to the balcony and that another legend about the brutality of Egon Bondy spread through The Academy of Applied Arts was something Vladimír learned about only a few days later.

Explosionalist Editions
Manuscript from October 10, 1951
1 original typescript on an Olivetti, 4 copies, February 2, 1952

LETTER TO ZBYNĚK FIŠER [EGON BONDY]

March 4, 1952

Dear Zbyněk,

Given you're acting like an old fart, I'll be a bit delicate in my language. You're exhibiting many of the signs of senility. One such sign is your difficulty in realizing that things exist outside your glorified presence. How can you hope to realistically capture the age when you lack so many of the necessary qualifications (to do this well). Though you try to make up for these shortcomings by reading, this is altogether inadequate if you fail to live. You might get on well with Říha, certainly better than I. He's stuffed himself with Surrealism and tends to be provincial like you. Those so-called excesses of yours are just complete bullshit if the circumstances working in your favor are taken into account. A shame you weren't born 20 years earlier. You might've been able to work through your paranoia. But the way you're going you'll only reach maybe two to five people who will give you a listen because they know it's a form of treatment for you. As is your fixation that you're interceding to inseminate Doctor's creative potency or mentor me! Are you oblivious to being a total waste of time? Any time I spend listening to you waxing philosophical, so full of yourself, means I have to work through the night to make up for it. I'm not entirely blaming you. We have different temperaments, but it's definitely a shame that for maybe half a year you couldn't be just on your own to pursue your own personal development. I have the way you talk more or less down (so you're not consumed by your usual vanity I won't mention your name when reproducing it since the core of this prattle represents a hundredth of the total verbal edifice). You should try to work. If I were to tell you that office secretaries effortlessly exercise their natural talents you would roar with laughter. But you are exactly the same. And then you go ballistic if anyone dare do something more than just indulge their nature. Yesterday I made plaster casts of Dočekal's and Jelínek's faces. It's a good thing Dočekal didn't know you earlier. It's likely he never would've written all those letters in which he so limpidly laid out the dilemmas faced by our generation, as he would've been too conflicted psychically before ever having the chance to express his inner growth. You're going to have to write a boatload, Zbyněk, if you expect to approach at least the quantity of his output. We can hardly talk about quality considering the scope of your and his thinking.

About that quantity, you could catch up if Mr. M. deigns to let you contribute. Please don't take this the wrong way, but I refuse to get involved. Spring is coming and beery debates no longer interest me.

Bouše and I and others have a slightly different makeup. If need be, we can fill the gaps in our knowledge, which you could fill for us, with one or two visits to the library. Maybe now you finally understand that Explosionalists have no need for the patronage of notorious epigones.

Mind the quality, Zbyněk, and don't be an imbecile. You should consider getting a herbarium.

How many times have you seen for yourself that I feel no need to superfluously flatter Doctor, and yet I have absolutely no doubt he could help you achieve 100x greater fame (sticking to your merits) than you would get by your own deserts. You came off as a know-it-all at the party, and I don't think you were playing the psychologist.

Regards,
Vladimír Boudník

THE STREET
(reportage)

I unlocked the garret's iron door that amidst the rust bore the remains of red paint and the partially effaced words, written in chalk: BEWARE EXPLOSIONALISM. A couple of feet in I stepped over the thick beam bordering the framework of roof timbers and took the hanging lock off the cracked door in the wooden partition covered by tar board and walked into a separate part of the attic.

Fitted with an iron handle, the glass skylight was opened in the same way you would raise a heavy umbrella over your head. The invited guests remained standing on the brick floor silently inert. Marysko was the first to break the stupor. He slowly stepped to the front wall forming a right-angled trapezoid, continually bending his head further back the closer he came to the object of his interest. It was an unfinished picture depicting a woman being strangled by a man.

"Well looky here . . . what sort of morbid picture is this?" — And while I was telling him about atavism and family stress, Dr. Hrabal went from one pile of clutter to the next, every now and then picking up some of the paper drawn or written on, then he sat down on the rug covering a mound of glass wool, knitted his hands together, and uttered, "Quite a place you've got here," — and he observed in the corner behind the chimney my selecting oil paints, folding and tying up the easel and tacking a quarto sheet of paper to the drawing board. I might've shown him how I used the etching press, but Doctor definitely did notice my herbarium improvised from two sheets of gray natural paper placed one on top the other with elderberry flowers and leaves and several tufts of wild grass affixed with tape peeking out . . .

Closing the skylight, we left the atelier painted in blue and pink and formerly occupied by a Gypsy family. Marysko forgot about the beam and tripped over it. He didn't regain his balance until being stopped by the plateless iron stove located under the other skylight, in this case one with broken glass so that when it was slushy out water would seep through onto the unraked ash.

As we were walking down the stairs I introduced Doctor to Hanes Reegen on the wall, gazing somewhere into the unknown . . .

We went out to the street. Dr. Hrabal was carrying the easel, and I was afraid he might poke someone in the eye. When we reached Malé náměstí, or Small Square, he remembered he hadn't picked up his choice allotment of lard. Having bought it, our conversation continued down Karlova Street, across Charles Bridge, up Mostecká Street, and under the arcade at Lesser Town Square.

I chose a support column with an outstanding cluster of blotches in the plaster, and while I was setting up the easel, Pepa (a sign painter) came up and affably greeted me: "Good day to you, Maestro, it's been awhile." "You know how it goes," I said apologetically, "one gets busy with stuff."

"Well, have a good one, I have to get going before they close on me." Pepa left, and as I consulted with Doctor about what I should begin to paint, Marysko wearily walked up and down the edge of the sidewalk.

> We agreed on a blot conjuring
> the image of a tree by a lake
> illuminated by moonlight.

I made a few brushstrokes, and a young woman walked up from the direction of St. Nicholas — the Baroque church. Doctor replied to her stunned face and timorous question in a modulated, gentle voice, as if he were speaking to a seven-year-old girl. The woman was pleasantly wonderstruck, and a moment later a man walked up who told us that at home they had a green tile stove and he was often amazed at the wealth of images the tiles' moiré evoked in his mind . . . The cellist Marysko informed us in a muffled voice that he was going for dinner . . .

As I continued to paint, more and more people stopped to look: a physician, workers, schoolchildren . . . the crowd grew. The physician asked: "What's the point of all this? To my mind, painting should depict beautiful, uncommon things, something not everyone can do. I have no idea what you're doing. What are you trying to achieve with this?" — I was a bit nervous, so my tone of voice became brusque:

"You don't understand because you have an aversion to anything new."

"Not at all, I would like to be edified, don't think me petty."

Dr. Hrabal answered the physician for me. He peppered his explanation with examples from art history. — — The number of onlookers grew. Two men in the crowd drew my attention. One was in a black overcoat and wearing glasses with dark frames, thick lips, and the other in a light-colored raincoat, sharp features, and perfectly slicked back graying hair, wearing a hat and a silk muffler. A host of people between me and them. The second of the two ironically opined so that everyone could hear:

"What you're doing is old hat and passé."

And I replied in the same tone: "You think I don't know that, and in those instances painting was done with an ass's tail."

"What? — — — !!!"

"I'm just relaying what I heard from a bystander here two weeks ago." The man in the raincoat turned his head to the crowd and unloaded: "He's a real beaut, isn't he? Black hat, long unruly locks, and *how do you do!*" and he disparagingly glared at me.

"I'm not shaving off my locks because of you." — "What?!" the man in the raincoat squeezed his way to me with the bespectacled man behind him . . . "what?! what locks?"

"I'm just repeating what you said. Surely you must know how to pronounce that *how do you do* more naturally than I. But if you're so interested, go buy me some pomade and I'll try to do my hair like yours!" He ignored my dig and pointed at the painting and asked: "What's this supposed to be?" I candidly warned him: "Don't smear it, it's oils." I said nothing about the subject. Over the original picture of a tree by a lake illuminated by moonlight were at least seven other sketches, and the whole gave the impression of a messy palette, a result of my involuntarily painting in turn what I saw in the blotches. "I'll tell you what you're doing. You're an agent provocateur!"

The man in glasses piped up and snorted: "This is fascist art!" I was about to fly off the handle, but I thought I saw Professor Slýž in the crowd, so I said nothing . . .

The graying man continued to attack. He asked an eleven-year-old boy: "Do you understand this?' and the boy truthfully answered, no. I defended myself: "Don't you think this is a shoddy way to gauge public opinion?" and I heard: "Look here, pack up your things and scram and be thankful that's all that happens." "If you have official authorization to intervene, then say so upfront. It's in poor taste and dishonest to speak like this to us if you have license to be hostile." The man in the light-colored raincoat reached his right hand into his left breast pocket. I was surprised that he pulled out a cigarette case instead of a badge. He turned it over in his hand a few times before he found the right position for it to be opened.

I told him as amiably as I could: *"Don't be nervous."*

"Ha ha, this guy is nuts, a typical demagogue . . . You know what? Let's discuss this like professionals! And I have to tell you straight off that what you're doing is vulgar dilettantism. It's a form of sexual perversion. . . . What's the meaning of this mess?"

"Look, about being a demagogue, I've sent hundreds of letters to dozens of places and I have yet to receive a single concrete response. Maybe you were one of the recipients, and if so, you had the chance to reply, and lastly: We've offered ourselves up to you as a target and you've been able to spew your bile at us so that you'll have peace of mind when you go home to the lap of your family. Now about this mess: I have a limited supply of quarto-sized paper and it soaks up the oil from the paints. Don't you think I'd be more comfortable lounging in a café instead of being here letting you insult me?" We argued fiercely for a while, and it was clear as day to me that my adversary would not relinquish the personal prestige he felt was his due. Since I still sensed Professor Slýž was watching me, I spoke as respectfully as I could. I also suspected that the man in the raincoat was a professor as well. I told him directly that the education system would certainly be grateful if he visited the schools to offer his professional advice. Or wasn't he aware of the difficulties and conflicts confronting students at art schools?

"That's pathetic. You fashion yourself a savior and martyr to boot."

Over his shoulder the head of his bespectacled companion popped up.

"Why aren't you working in a factory?"

"Don't divert our people from reality!"

"Street life isn't reality? You know what, why don't you go to the relevant office and arrange an official permission for me to draw at my workplace. As for myself, I submitted a formal request three months ago and still haven't received an approval."

"So what you're doing here is Surrealism, is that it?!" condescendingly said the uncouth highbrow in the hat, "I mean, what is this supposed to depict?"

"Nothing," I said in resignation.

The interrogator portentously looked at his wristwatch and announced: "Good people, remember this historic moment. At 6:35 p.m. this genius here created for you NOTHING."

My eye fell on the figures of two police officers, and I saw one grab his holster, likely to keep the pistol from falling out as he took off running somewhere . . .

A smaller, younger man joined in the discussion. He was stocky and his hair was parted on the side. He exclaimed: "Comrades, comrades, this is simply not the way to go about it. Don't argue. What will foreigners say?" A car honked. Those who couldn't fit under the arcade were standing two meters deep in the street. No one paid the young man any mind. He was vainly trying to assist his voice by gesturing wildly. A moment before Dr. Hrabal had left the group he'd been talking with and was now standing at my left side. The graying man in the hat torturously watched me spread another layer of paint on the paper. "Don't be nervous," he sarcastically threw back at me. "You, sir, are just repeating my words. And anyway, I've got a reason to be nervous." Dr. Hrabal also chimed in and was irately put on notice: "You should watch yourself, too. You're also a dubious character." Doctor was having none of it and self-confidently buried the man in an avalanche of learning. Fiddling with the collar of the moralizing fop's raincoat, he came across as more heartfelt than his interlocutor was prepared to recognize. The man tried to step back but bumped against a wall of human bodies.

He screamed in disgust: "Don't touch me. I have no idea who the heck you are!" and in a minute delivered his verdict: "Judging from the way you speak, you're a lawyer, aren't you?"

An ingenuous looking woman stood up for us: "Why don't you leave them alone, they're not hurting anyone." Others also took my side, and one guy confirmed that not too long ago he saw me make some fine pictures from blotches, for instance a face bent over a microscope. He said you can't expect it to be as good as that every time out. I caught sight of Pepa in the crowd . . .

A moment earlier the policeman who'd run off returned with backup. Four police officers silently observed us from the opposite sidewalk.

The debate no longer followed any logical course. The crowd of a hundred (maybe two hundred) spectators fragmented into dozens of smaller discussion groups. Names from Rembrandt to Mánes to Picasso echoed in the air. The names of art movements from Primitivism to Surrealism . . . A policeman crossed the street, looked at his watch, and ordered: "You have two minutes to pack up and leave." All those people in the street alone made me nervous, and I was happy to have the situation resolved. So I didn't argue, and while I was packing up the painting implements and the easel, Doctor matter-of-factly informed the crowd that I get up every day before 4 a.m. to take the bus to Kladno to work at the steel mill, and come back to Prague in the afternoon. Our adversaries blushed.

The young man with the parted hair suggested: "Come with me," and parried the accusations that he was summoning us in an official capacity by saying he was an editor.

We left. On Charles Bridge, near the plaque commemorating St. John of Nepomuk being tossed into the river, I tossed that painted quarto of paper into the Vltava. The editor whimpered: "Why did you throw it away? What a shame!"

I felt odd. I was watching a man walking in front of us thinking it was Professor Slýž. At the bridge tower I caught up to greet him: "Good evening, Professor." He groaned: "I'm not a professor." "Sorry, have a nice night."

The editor, Doctor, and I turned and walked in the direction of the National Theater. The editor was speaking in the tone of a benevolent teacher. He was convinced we were sly pranksters. I demonstrated that I was serious about what I was doing, and as proof, today was at least the seventieth time I'd painted on the street, and I explained the meaning behind our actions and the participation of the wider public. We were thirsty, so Doctor and I decided to pop into U Fleků. Our friend from the street was reluctant at first, saying he didn't drink, but then accepted the invitation. The conversation continued over 10° dark lager. And like a good comrade, Doctor shared his ration of lard with us.

The editor — a Moravian as well as a student at the Communist Party's College of Politics — was pestering us as to why we didn't tackle the whole matter scientifically. Doctor presented examples from the Bible, but after several reservations, usually beginning with, "Well of course, fellows, but . . . ," Doctor shifted to the domain of concrete life, and in the end this young Moravian lad, scientifically buried under materialist rationales, took refuge in laughter. Toppled over in his chair, he ambiguously pointed an accusatory finger at us — *you — you!*

Then he became more serious and remarked that perhaps I should write something for him and he would do his best to get it published, and then more sheepishly he added: "I'm not looking for fame, but if you happened to break through then wouldn't my name also be mentioned?"

When on October 27, 1950, I lay on the rug covering the bed of glass wool and extinguished the kerosene lamp, I nearly had a panic attack and convulsions under the flood of additional thoughts, and for a long time I argued with the phantasms of my naysayers over what I'd failed to express this evening.

Explosionalist Editions
1 original typescript on an Olivetti, 5 copies, March 7, 1952

MAN IS AN ODD CREATURE

Man is an odd creature. He's kept up at night by the conviction that this is the right moment to unburden himself to the world of everything that's tormenting him. These are states of idiocy. All he needs to do is get dressed and go out to the street. The agonizing sentences keep gnawing at his mind. Humanity! Yet the man standing with a woman in the passageway has other problems. He asks: "Where were you? Tell me! Have you no shame! . . . your sick mother lying at home . . . and in the cinema? Liar!" And the two figures rave at each other, one channeling lies and the other jealousy. Superenergy! . . . A man in a leather coat pushing a broken-down motorcycle couldn't care less, given his situation, what anyone else is thinking. Art pipeline! . . . The hand of someone possessing a doltish face drawing on the wall of a dimly lit bathroom the symbol of female genitalia could give a rat's ass if it corresponds to acceptable standards of taste . . . One man, an enterprise director, kisses his father's hand because years ago he whipped him unconscious with a riding crop, all because he had wanted to study at the art academy. The father was right. And now that the son is lord and master he could draw whenever he felt like it, if he wanted, but he's the director and is unable to. Years ago the director's father was an object of derision to the young. And today? Memories of the lives of this or that paragon fade or are blotted out in the minds of the young, and the words of the director's father find fertile ground as they did in our grandmothers' era. Charles IV had a court jester, and so many people today wish to obtain one as well! So many people today wish to tell their neighbor: "You, sir, are an ignoramus and a cretin!" while quite aware of the impact such honesty will have

— but say it they must — and here their eyes, accustomed to religious paintings, take umbrage at a picture that does not comply with their tastes. Ha! An idiot must've made this! And if they see a painter at work? What's this supposed to be? Why are you sketching the roof of St. Nicholas in charcoal when it's green? . . . adding their only "original" quip: "My 5-year-old son could've made this!! — Why don't you paint like Mánes?" The painter asks what he knows about Mánes? The person admonishing him tries to divert the conversation to Dutch still lifes. "Fine," says the painter, "but what do you find so appealing about Mánes?" The instigator "momentarily" cannot remember anything Mánes painted, and anyway, where does this kitschmonger get off questioning folks like this. An artist should be humble. Yes, that's what I'm always reading. Why is he promoting his work himself??! His art will be vindicated on its own if it's legit. Ha ha! What a joke. Go have a look at old masters, that fruit, that drapery. NO! Today's artists aren't worth a damn!

Explosionalism
1952

LETTER TO OFFICIAL ARTISTS AND ART CRITICS

July 1, 1955
Prague

Dear Official Artists (Painters) and Art Critics!

Forgive me for writing to you today about matters that will come to your attention from many quarters in the coming years.

You shall be condemned for having remained emotionally and often consciously unresponsive to developments and the objective exigencies of the age, for having made the visual arts into a passive vocation and refusing to use the opportunity when presented to undertake an exhaustive analysis of the laws governing creativity, for having expedited, without deeper understanding, the transition from formalistic isms to realism, for having been impotent to prevent the ennui of the general public under the sway of artworks created for personal gain, for not having corrected the antiquated conventional thinking that has led to "art" studios being set up in enterprise offices and in factories, for having poorly grasped when society might be disposed toward active art for self-realization, and thereby you have automatically created an art only for a narrow circle of people, hankering for the prestigious, to distinguish yourselves from previous generations, which you have maligned (I am excluding illustrators from this critique).

You shall be condemned for having failed to comprehend that the task of the artist is to communicate and in so doing to attenuate social conflicts, frequently a consequence of an egocentric, narrow-minded insularity or a cravenly cautious conveyance of reality, for having wanted to make visual artists normal people by suppressing their essence ("normal" in how perceptions are received) without understanding that such normality is conceivable only during a period of economic boom when blanket orders are filled (analogous to a factory that wants to start manufacturing high-demand products and gives priority to engineers who are routinists over those prone to experiment), for having been oblivious to how film, literacy, photography influence the creative process and the elevation of human imagination, for not having noticed practically scientifically intelligible outcomes, for having noticed the largely inactive person, for having persisted in the presumption that you were seeding reality, whose course would virtually be the same absent your interventions, for having failed to comprehend that it's often easier to learn to imitate photography (and without any demands on creative genius) than it is to learn how to work a lathe.

You shall be condemned for not having seen the consistent principles found both in creative activity and in the development of new technical thinking. An absence of cooperation has held back both disciplines, although in the technical field there is a scientific awareness of this fact, while in the realm of officially sanctioned art, isolated from the public by barriers, complexes, and a paucity of information, and thus far ignored by this public, fallacious values continue to be adhered to for their own sake.

You shall be condemned for not having conducted a broad discussion on the arts, for having become stagnant and squandered energy on the single-minded liquidation of formalism without grasping that the luxuriant life of the present would render the old formalism a relic of the past even without your overdone admonitions. (Many a liquidator of the old formalism has introduced a new formalism.)

It shall be demonstrated that you have hypocritically inveigled people even in those cases when their creativity was utterly neglected within the purview of official art, and conversely, that you have belittled the natural, robust creativity of ordinary folk, that you have failed to notice, or denied, that once barriers are removed people are capable on the basis of free association of creating pictures from blotches on plaster façades etc., and are capable of having a rich, tangible psychic and physiological experience, that you have failed to observe that this method gives the ordinary person the capability to create daily, per individual needs, many more images than the whole academy might produce in a full day of work.

In effect, human imagination today competes with the work of photographers, filmmakers, and industrial designers, as the latter combines taste and utility.

It wouldn't be right to condemn you for having ignored Explosionalism in the press for so many years, because the existence of this movement was and is not tied to a few individuals expressing only what interests them, on the contrary, expressions of this kind would have crippled Explosionalism over the past years and reduced the receptivity of its adherents to those thousands who were instrumental in fortifying the movement through their sincere, even if at times crude, interest.

Vladimír Boudník
Jana Želivského 35, Prague XI

MANIFESTO NO. 3 : EXPLOSIONALISM

March 2, 1956

The mission of Explosionalism seven years after issuing Manifesto No. I is at heart identical with the mission as then expressed.

This is: With respect to visual art, to eliminate barriers to the active involvement of people in a process of co-creation, to eliminate from the brain ossified opinions and prejudices, to mark out a rightful place for imagination in the creative process, and to vindicate it from accusations of being pathologically unhealthy, given that films, photography, literacy, and a plethora of illustrated material surrounding humanity have impacted the brain (including the cerebral cortex) to produce the mental and physical ability to now create on the basis of free association objectively bona fide pictures (from blotches), given that the scientific understanding of causes has directed creative work toward values that afford a complex overview of the creative potency of a humanity liberated from the hegemony of automatic lines, which otherwise is an unreliable way to reproduce mental images. This reality will obligate professional artists to elevate their work to an extremely high level, free themselves from academist craft, and form a connection to peak experiences, activities, and currents of thought of present-day human society. Otherwise — given the parity of the viewer's mental creative power — mere craftsmanship will be the only thing at which they excel.

In view of the conservative insularity of active professional artists, the potential for the general public's provisional self-sufficiency also cannot be excluded. Since we know that blotches on their own, or a blotch enhanced by additional drawing, triggers in the viewer, in accordance with the second signal system, real psychic processes more or less equal to the psychic processes elicited by realistic paintings in the older sense of the word, all the viewer need do is photograph or put a frame around a given blotch cluster found on a wall.

It is known that the qualitative development of the cerebral cortex is closely connected to environmental influences (the intensity of environmental influences is understandably contingent on the disposition of a person at the time these influences are active).

Today it is absolutely malignant that the conservative consciousness passed down from previous generations isolates this imaginative aptitude cultivated in the brain on grounds that it is aberrant perception, for we need to keep in mind that preceding generations lacked on average the monumental stimuli and influences of today. During seven years of experimentation by Explosionalists with many thousands of active participants, the opposite was proved, that it is aberrant and unhealthy for brain function to continue to resist said activity. Naysayers who deny the potential for positive results are correct if we take into account the impossibility of affecting uninformed people for the length of time necessary to overcome their inhibitions. A half hour of stimulation is usually enough time on average to penetrate the brain of an informed person to bolster the accumulated proclivities for qualitative change.

Explosionalists chose the form of direct contact with people on the street and in the workplace. The process of consciousness raising, with dozens or hundreds of active participants, was extremely rapid in each individual.

Explosionalists have surmounted prior isms through a synthesis of viewpoints, and thereby facilitated the generation of intelligibility between work and the picture. (Peremptory detractors, with a rated load of superstition, are impervious to interpretation due to their long years of holding a distorted view of the problem.)

We have verified that these detractors reject with equal bluster the reality of physiological and psychological findings, such as on the second signal system and conditioned reflexes. Such detractors also reject the technological progress achieved during their adult lifetimes, and in some cases they do not accept the reality of a breakthrough or the capability of hundreds of people to successfully achieve it.

The people of today possess the ability to create a tsunami of evidence on the makeup of their inner psychic world, formed by objective exterior stimuli (including complex mutual relationships).

Explosionalist thinking is similar to a nuclear chain reaction of radioactive isotopes, and by interacting with the imagination manages, in a matter of minutes, to transform the blotches on a building's wall into a picture gallery. And this has surpassed that coterie who are limited to comparing the relative potency of art made by hand to that of photography.

We have entered an era when a few minutes of active imagination competes with the work of cinema, as the picture has ceased to be a snapshot and instead has become an explosive chain reaction of conscious mental images. Given that the cave drawings prehistoric man made 30,000 years ago include a rather large number of top-notch works of art, how much more prolific could the work of contemporary humans be when their lives are interconnected in an infinite web of relationships. It is unsound to leave the expression of contemporary life's complexity to only a chosen few.

Furthermore:

The objective photographs of our planet taken by aircraft and rockets in the stratosphere have ushered in a new relationship with the spatial organization of the picture. By virtue of the human brain's spatial qualities, Explosionalists proliferate to the boundless reaches of our planet, where imagination will be an important, active factor as the sense of our planet's smallness will be negated, a sense spawned by advancements in transportation technologies and signaling devices, including television and radio.

Even ten-thousandth of a millimeter, enlarged by an electron microscope, provides the impetus to create a picture. Human imagination alters the basic relationship to objects. We know that photography's value is that it allows one to visualize, during the active participation of receptors (eyes and their attendant nerves), with absolute exactness something that happened in the past, to mentally experience it without having to rely on dreams, fevered hallucinations, or old-age reveries, which tend to be predominated by perceptions from early youth. Explosionalism enables one to experience an endless chain of past imaginings in a form that accords with the immediate disposition and channeling ability of the intellect — after attaining equilibrium — to accept a new reality. People will have the ability to psychically develop over their whole lives and to adapt to progress.

We should stress that this is nothing new. Explosionalists were influenced by folk imagination (the reading of molten lead, conceiving names for flowers, rocks, clouds, etc.). We subsequently verified that Paleolithic cave paintings, the works of Leonardo da Vinci, Goya, Victor Hugo, were created through free association, as has the whole avalanche of work from contemporaneous painters. But none of this previous work altered in any way the consciousness of the public at large. In practice, association served as a poor medium, or as an exclusive activity that often sufficed alone for the smug myth of individual achievement to take root.

Experiments with around 7,000 individuals have demonstrated to us that in the first minutes over 90% thought the whole thing dubious, didn't understand it, or viewed it through the lens of folk superstition (reading molten lead, etc.) without making any effort to expand their attitudes beyond the static and fixed.

Over the following minutes new attitudes on the question quickly formed synergistically with the accumulated energies in the unconscious, which is ample confirmation of people's natural, objectively valid capabilities.

Detractors who claim that Explosionalism neglects objective reality are mistaken. The opposite is true! It is wedded to and contingent on reality. Besides, it's impossible to see in blotches an object or event that we have not internalized from the real world.

The frequent strangeness of forms and actions is a result of accumulated images, often formed at different times, combined with immediate stimuli (blotches). It reflects a person's more advanced nervous system.

Vladimír Boudník

LETTER TO BOHUMIL HRABAL

September 30, 1963

Dear Doctor,

I hope you don't mind my writing to you. It was really great to see you again after so many years. Eight years ago you were a true pillar of support for my work and one of the few who believed it wasn't entirely pointless. Just last year my endeavors were misrepresented to outrageously malign me, and as a consequence many now see me as a borderline lunatic. Even though I have suffered a great deal emotionally, I've never wavered from my path as an artist. And for me this is infinitely more gratifying than any peace of mind snitching might offer. At most that would be an official form of satisfaction with fleeting psychological impact on my life.

Please accept the enclosed catalogue from my exhibition in Warsaw last year.

Warm regards,
Vladimír Boudník
Kostnické náměstí 5, Prague 3

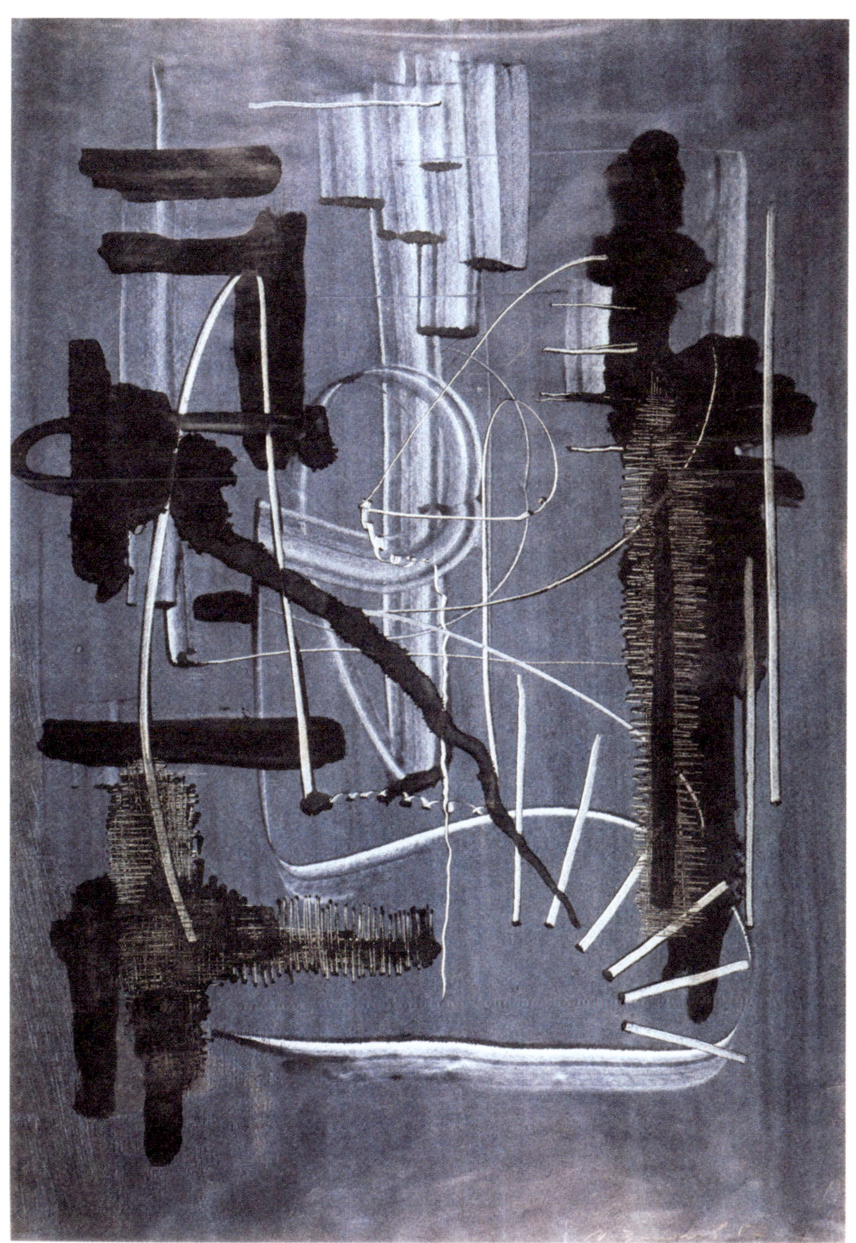

Untitled, from a planisher, monotype, 1957

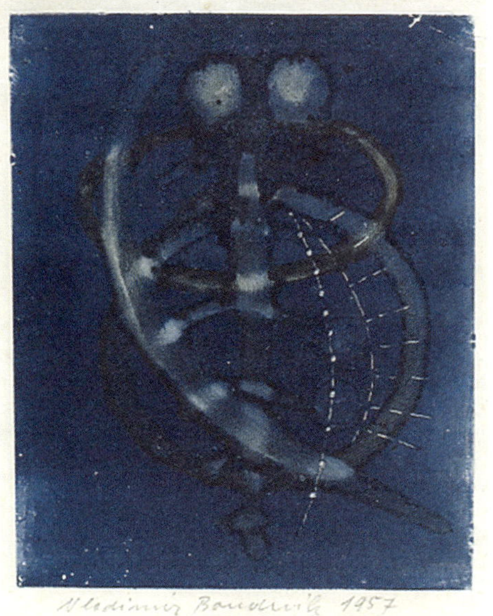

Untitled, monotype, 1957

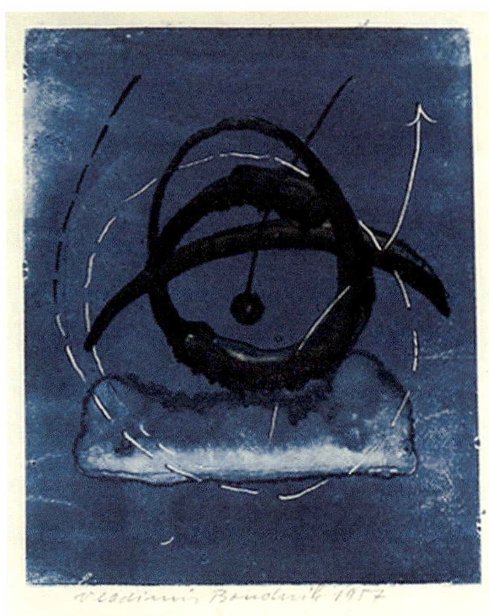

Untitled, monotype, 1957

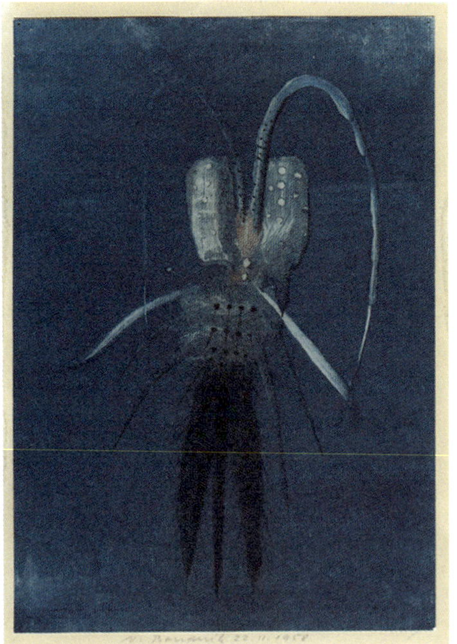

Jellyfish, monotype, 1958

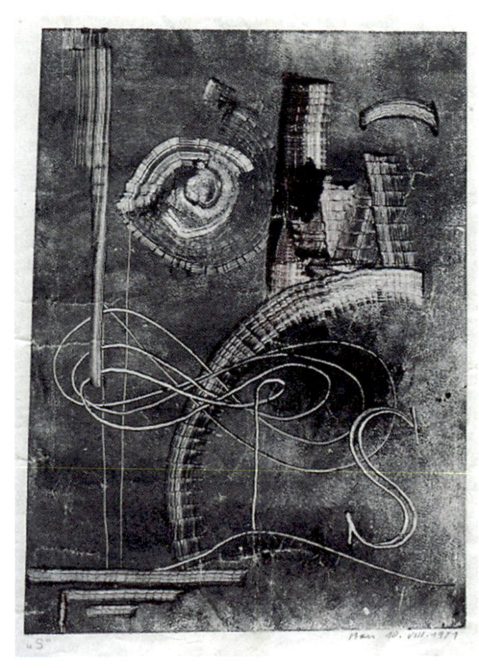

S, monotype, 1951

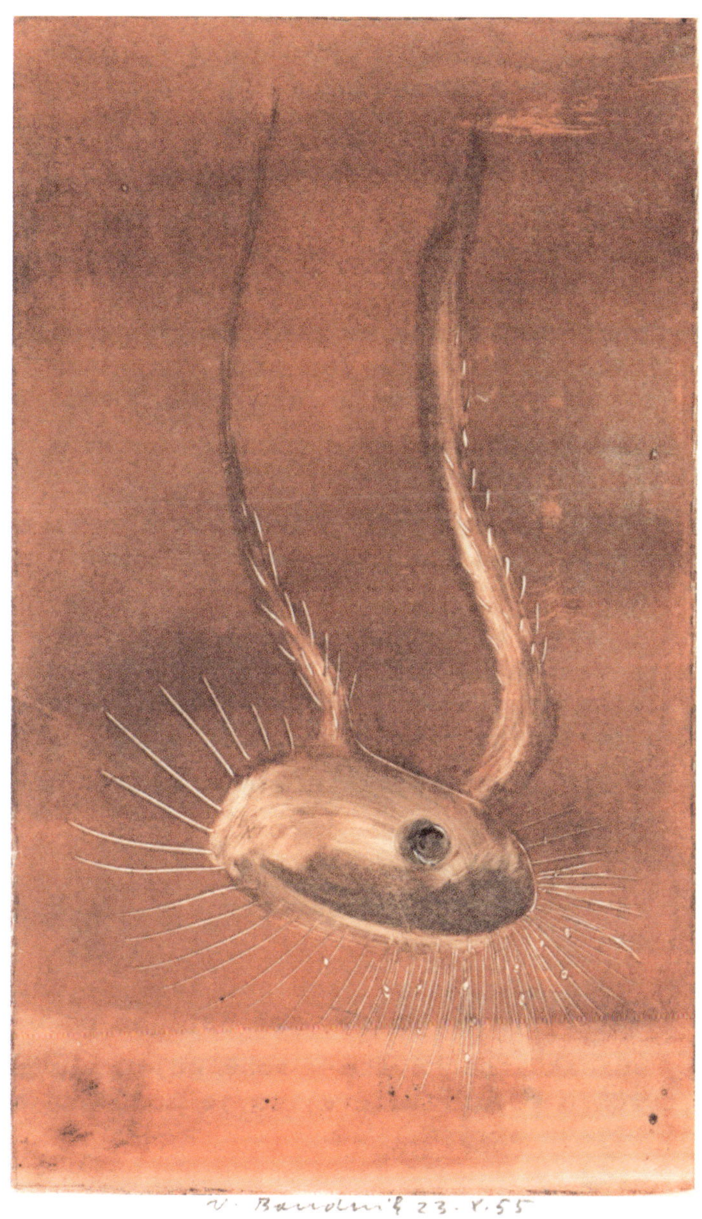

Jellyfish, monotype, 1955

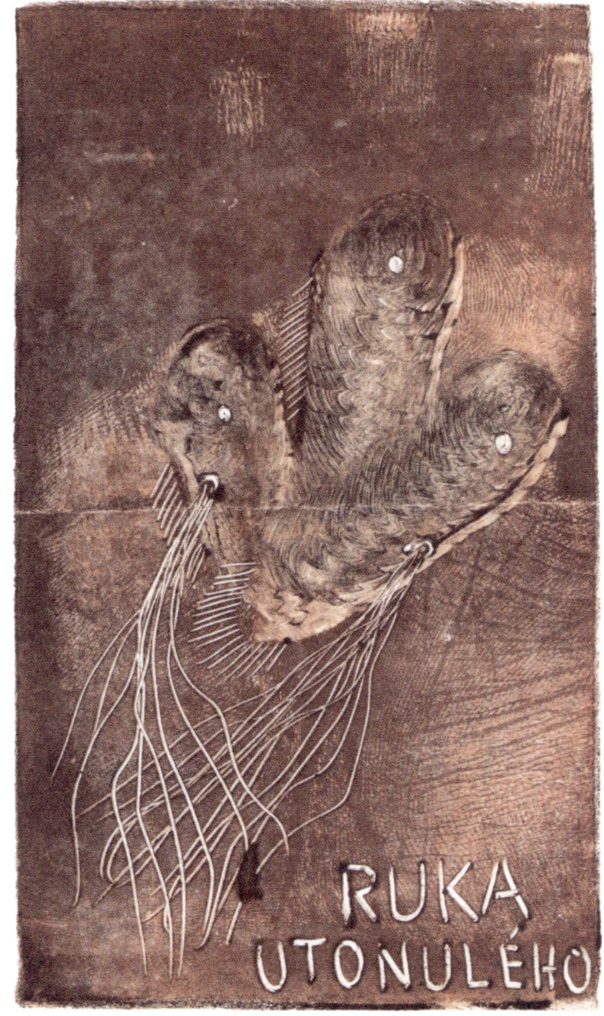

Hand of Drowned Man, monotype, 1955

Dead Deep-sea Fish, monotype, 1955

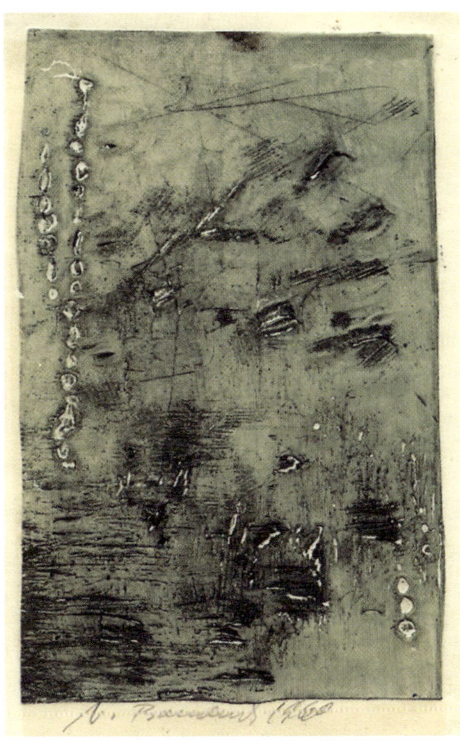

Coral Reef, active print, 1960

Undersea Reef, active print, 1960

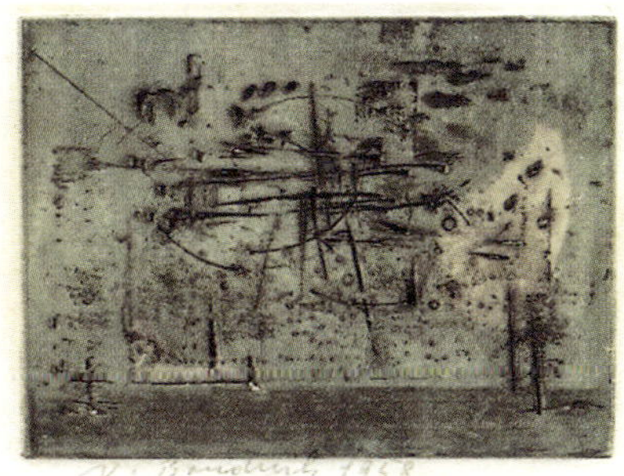

Untitled, active print, 1958

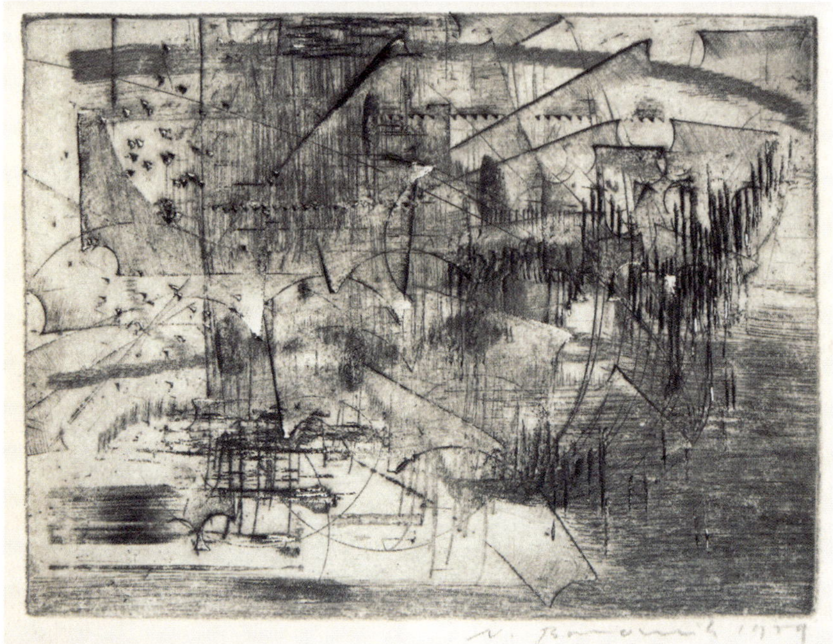

City-Factory, drypoint & active print, 1959

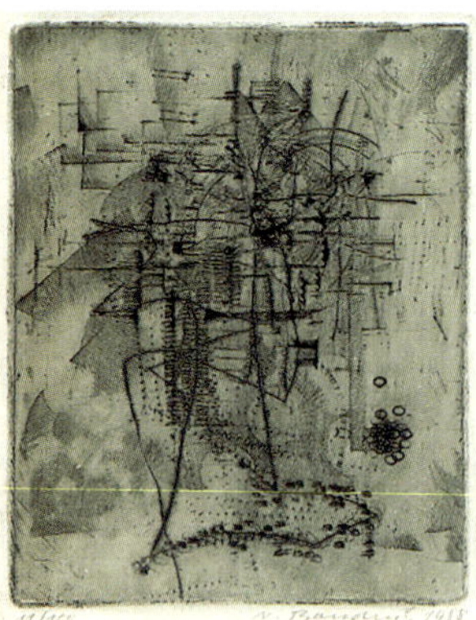

Untitled, active print, 1958

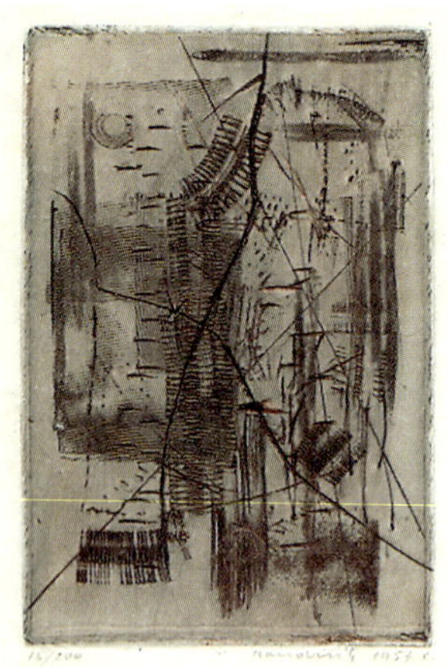

Explosionalism, active print, 1957

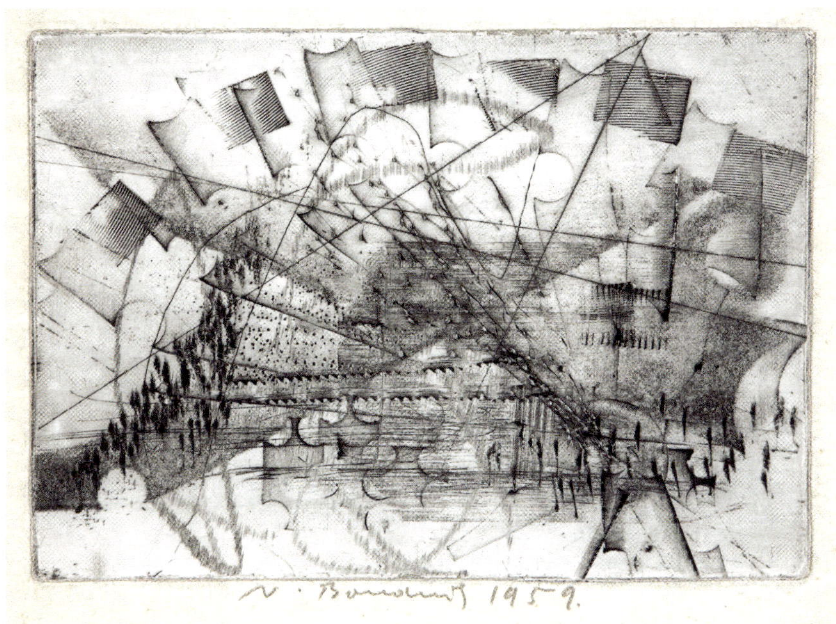

Material Traces, active print, 1959

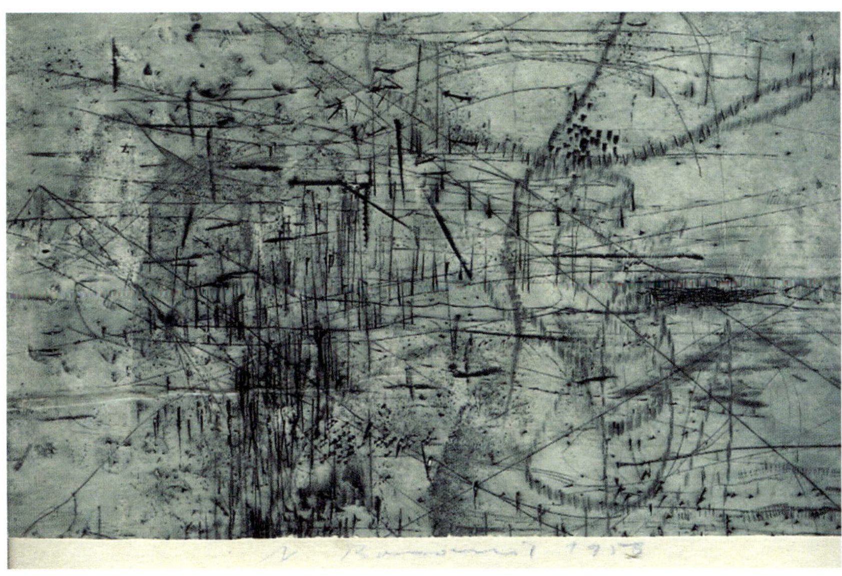

Machine Traces, active print, 1958

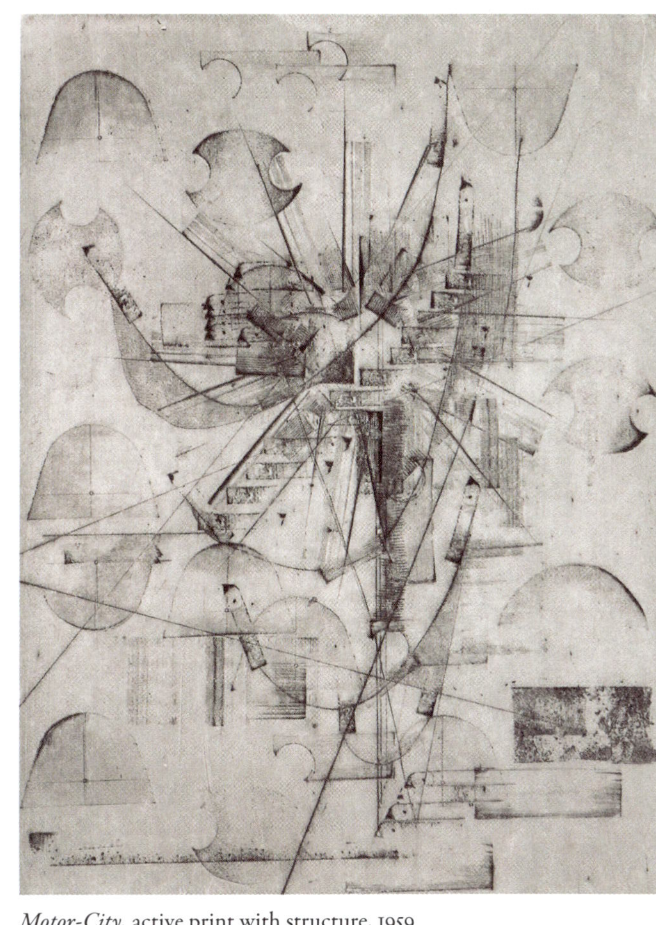

Motor-City, active print with structure, 1959

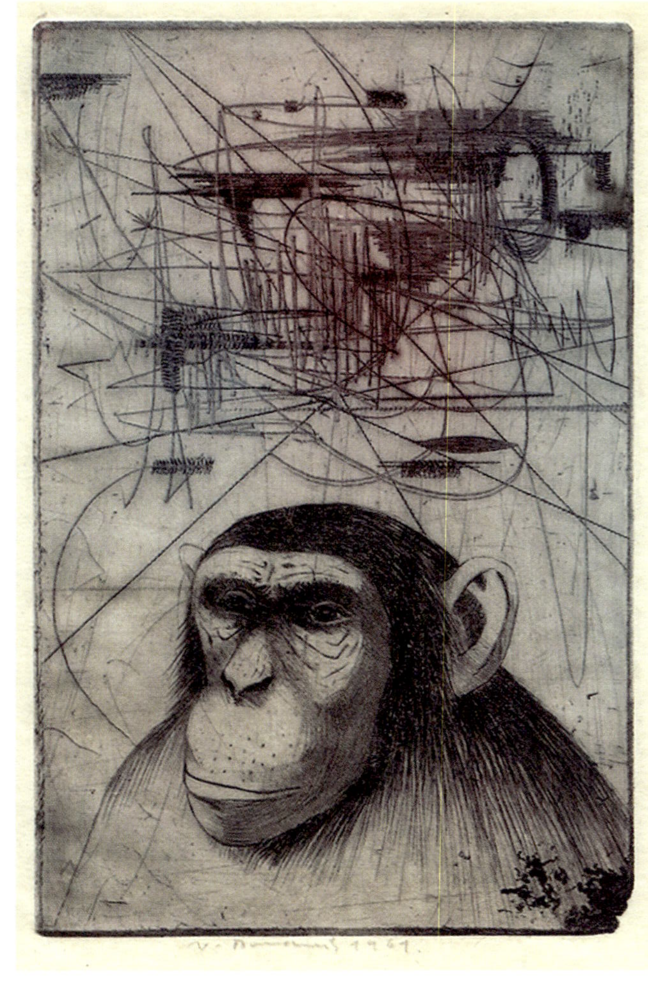

Chimpanzee, drypoint with active method, 1961

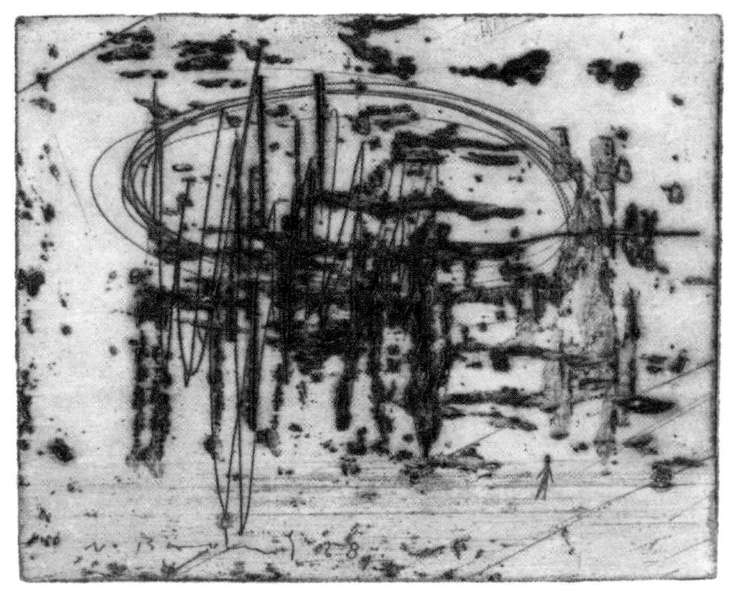

Oval with Figure, active print, 1958

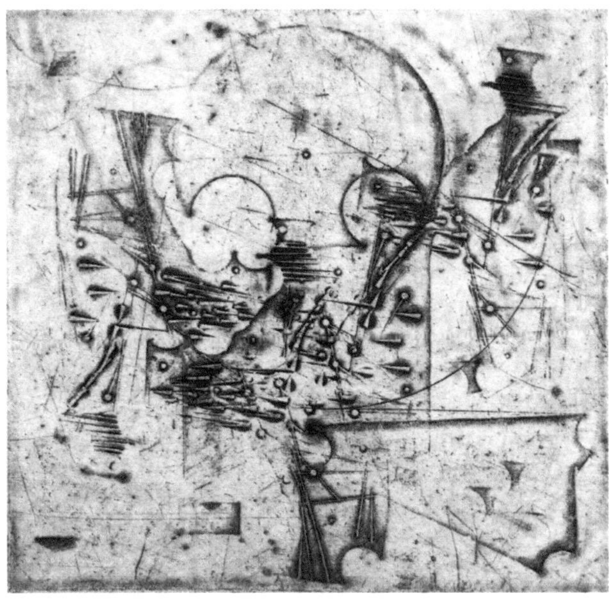

Skull, drypoint & active print, 1960

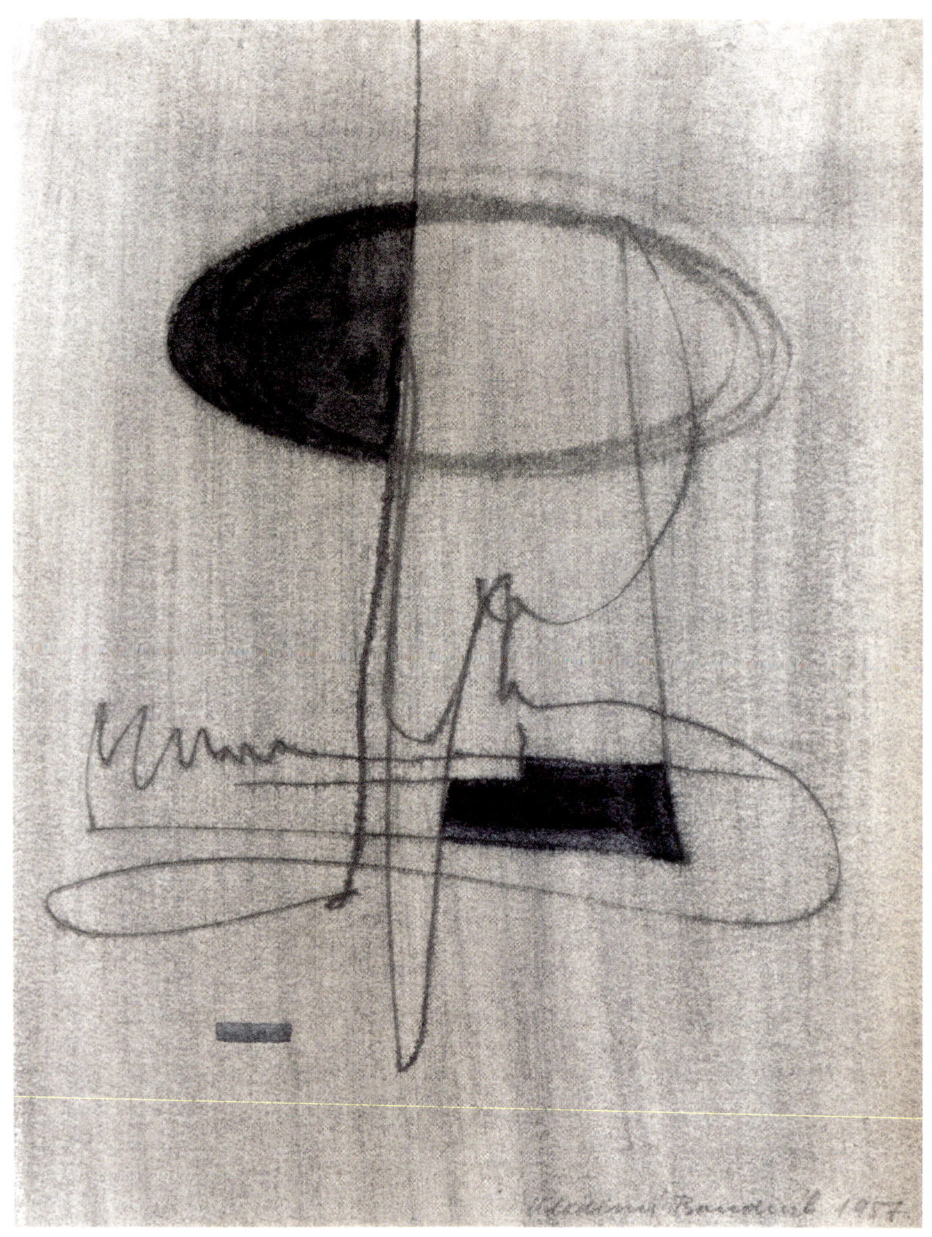

Seismograms of Impulses, grattage, 1957

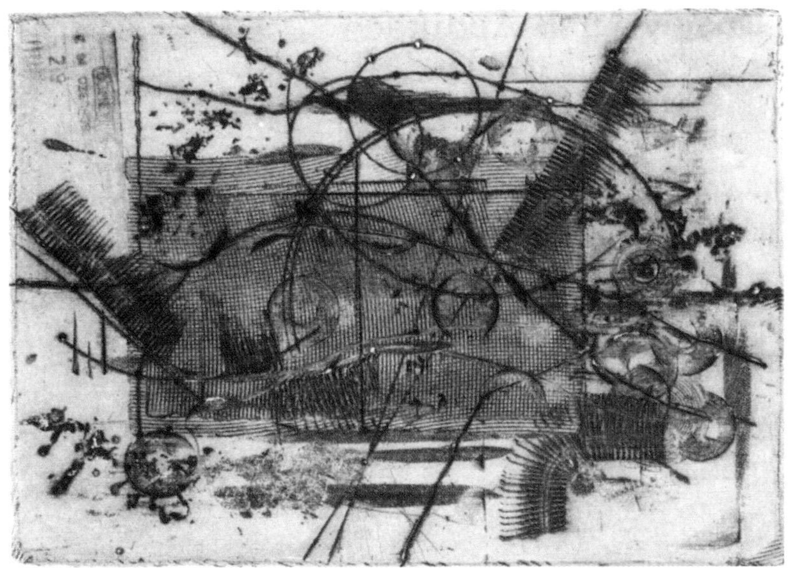

Untitled, active print, 1958

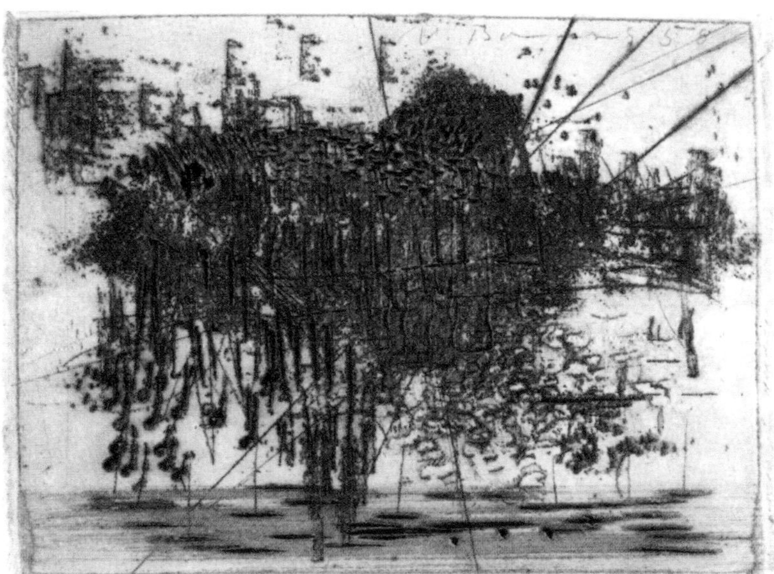

Radioactive Fish, active print, 1958

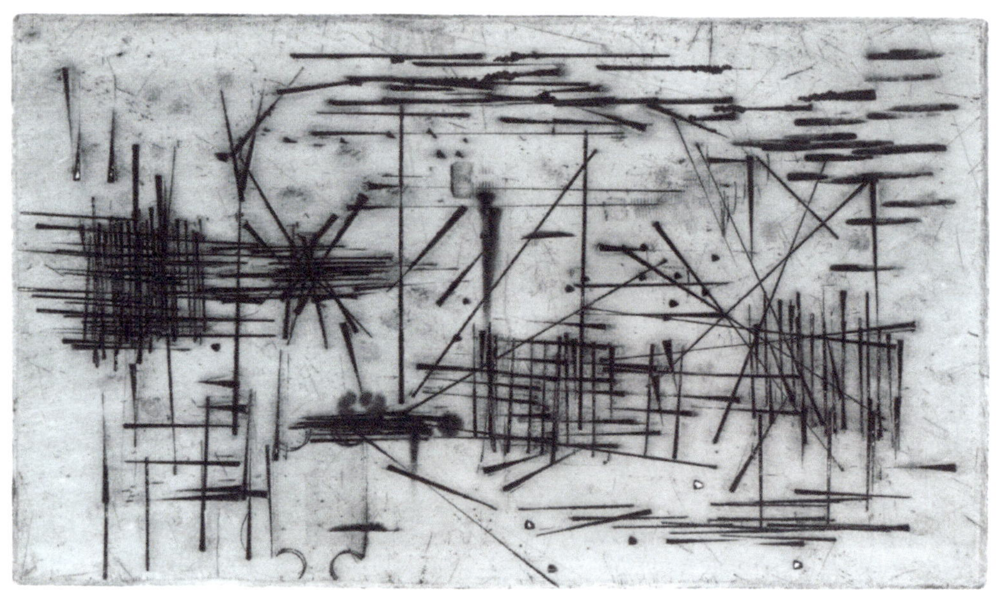

Cosmic Blast, active print, 1960

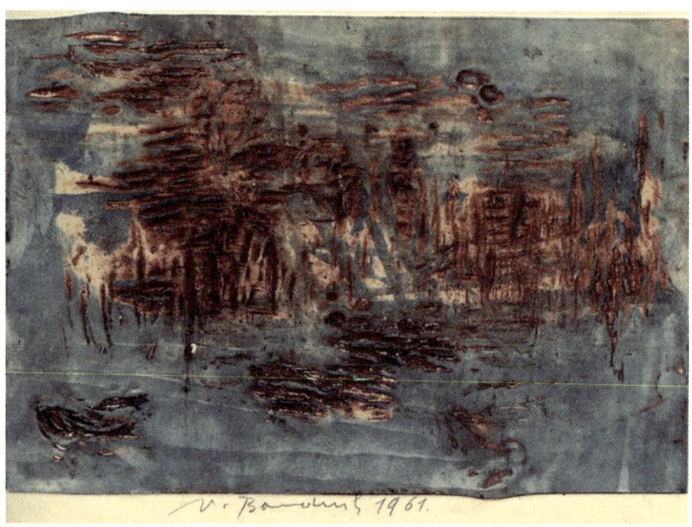

Untitled, active print, 1961

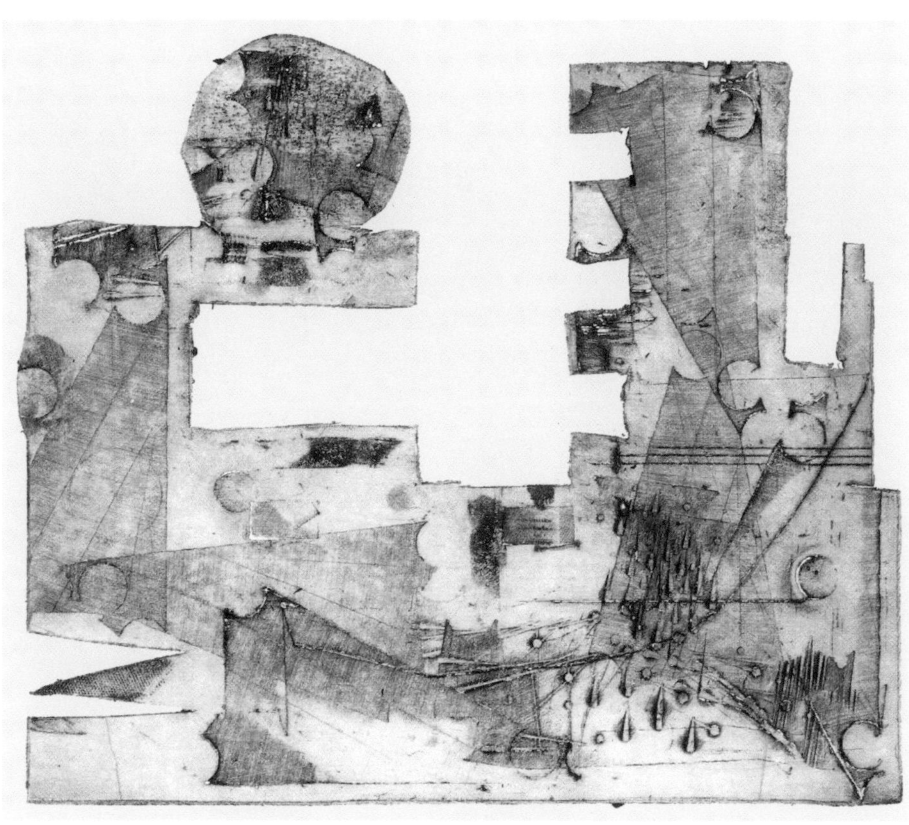

Untitled, unconventional format, active print, 1960

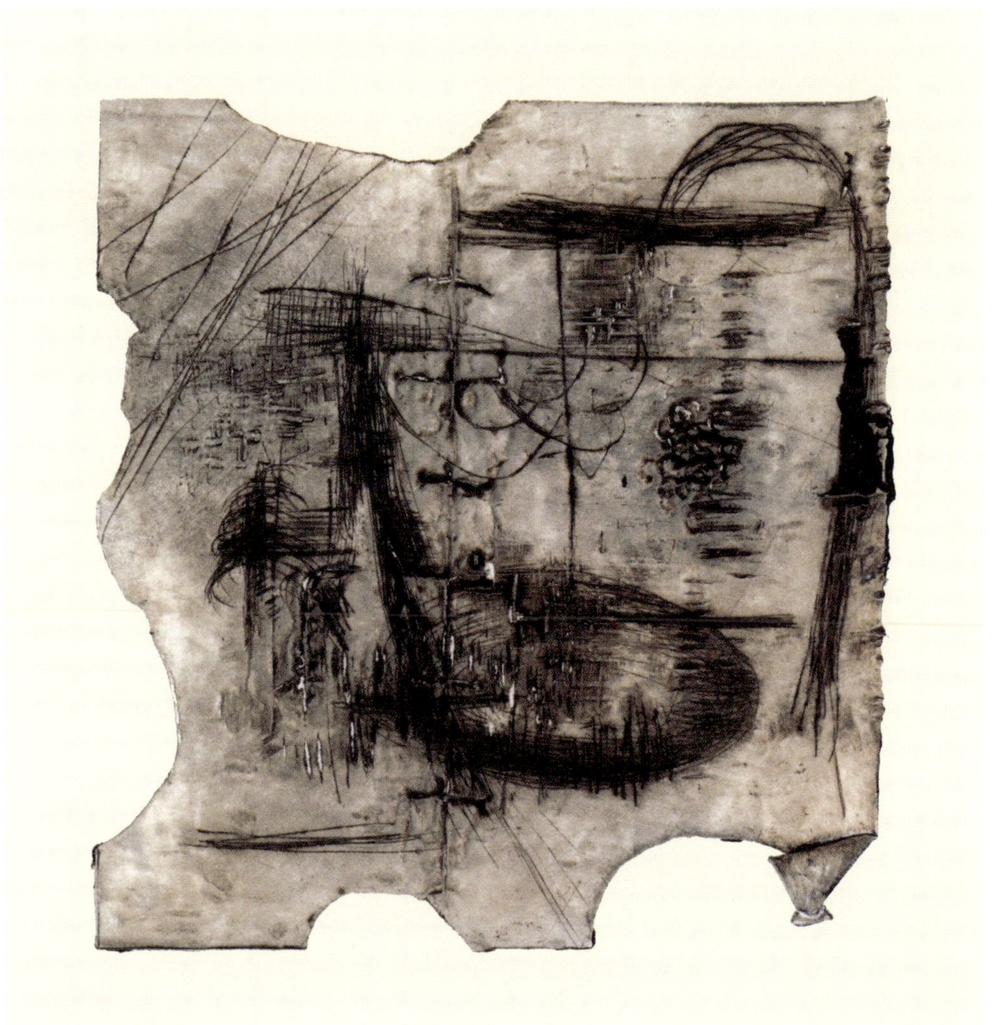

Untitled, unconventional format, active print, 1960

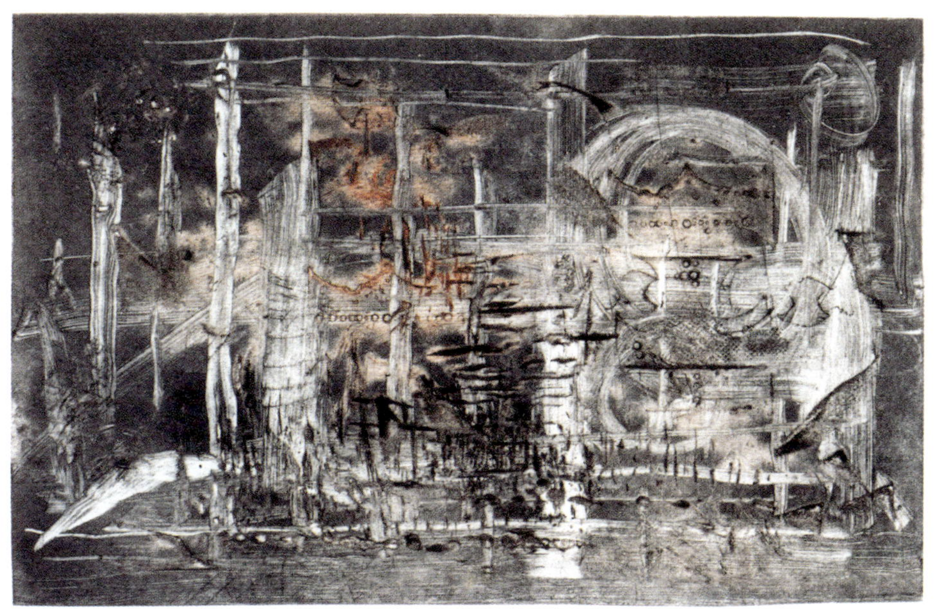

For Ivanka, monotype & active print, 1965

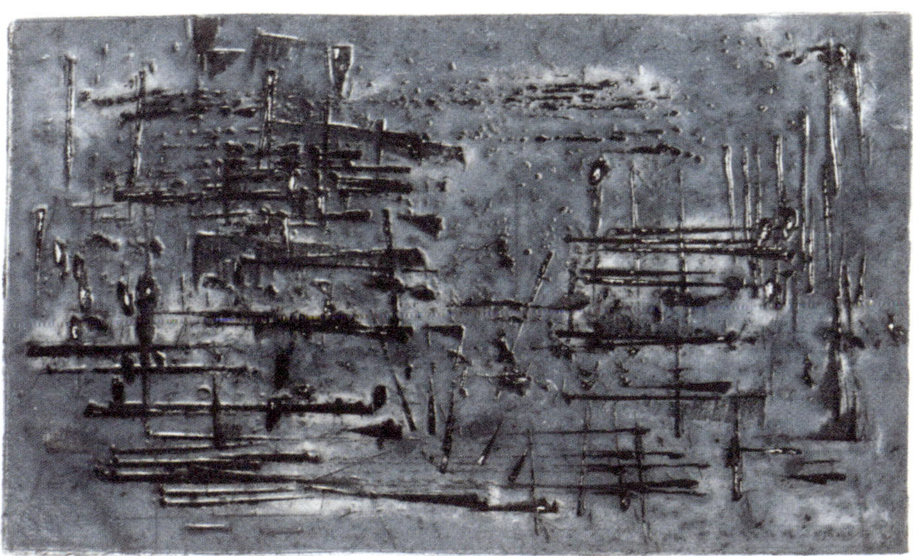

Machine Traces, active print, 1965

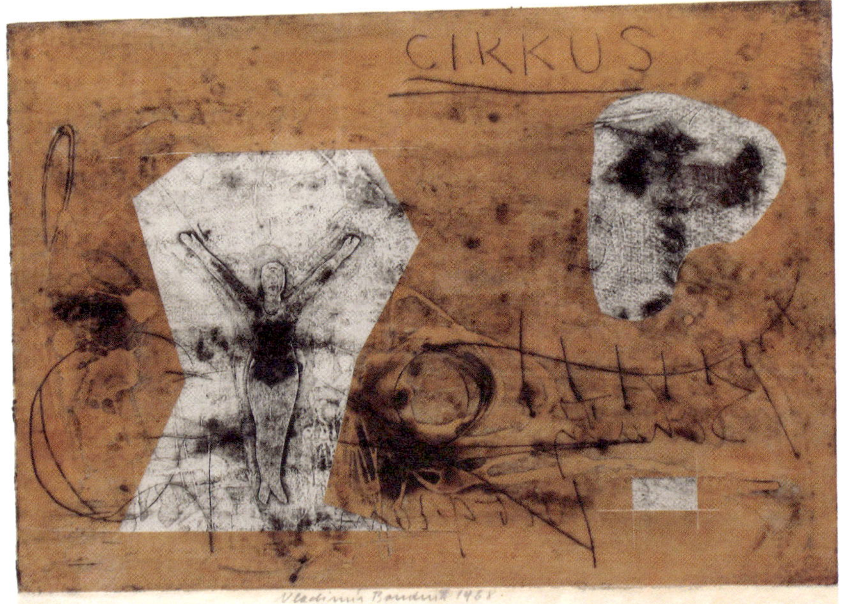

Circus, collage & active print, 1968

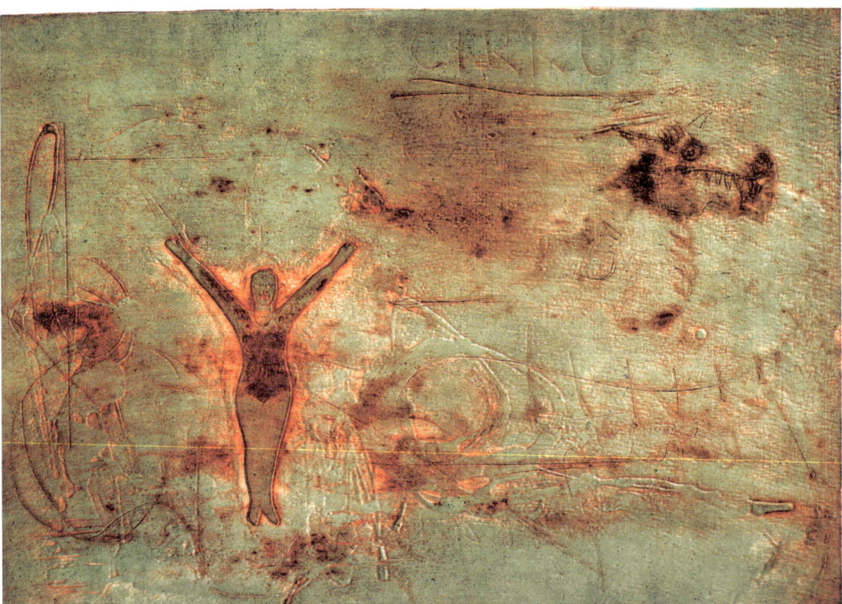

Circus, active print, 1968

The collection of "pedagogic texts" Bohumil Hrabal wrote to celebrate Vladimír Boudník's life came about under peculiar circumstances. In Czechoslovakia at that time a new group of fanatic communists had come to power, and they began to brutally meddle in the lives of the country's citizens. This period, called "normalization," was a pointless step backward that affected all aspects of society, including culture. Hrabal, already a famous writer by then, could not publish during this period. Exhibitions of a progressive artist such as Vladmír Boudník were banned. As a reaction to this nationwide predicament the underground and samizdat publications emerged.

The Vladimír Boudník Friendship Society, an unsanctioned association, took as its mission the promotion and dissemination of the recently deceased graphic artist's ideas and work. The Society organized a Tribute to Vladimír Boudník to commemorate what would've been his fiftieth birthday in 1974. A selection of his diary was to be published under the title *One-Seventh*, and a host of former colleagues were invited to contribute something. Hrabal's piece was on point. He wrote "Diary Written at Night" as a poetic description of how "One-Seventh" came into being when he and Boudník lived together and were virtually inseparable. A samizdat edition with texts from Boudník, Hrabal, and myself was published in May 1974 in a run of 200 copies, 50 of which were numbered and included 16 reproductions of artwork. Before work on the Tribute was complete, in the fall of 1973, Hrabal stated that, "while I was writing this text so many memories came flooding back to me of those years spent with tender barbarians

Vladimír and Egon Bondy that I just had to keep writing."

At the beginning of 1974, an exhibition of Boudník's prints was held in Ústí nad Orlicí, and for the occasion Hrabal wrote "Letter to Those Attending a Vernissage" and read it out at the opening. It was likewise included in the catalogue. Hrabal combined these pages with the typescripts of the two previous texts, threw in "Abdication," had it bound, and a handful of copies of the first samizdat edition of *The Tender Barbarian* were in the world. The following dedication appears in one of them: *To the Vladimír Boudník Friendship Society, Hrabal, February 7, 1974.*

The Comfort Society [Spolek Pohodlí] also received a copy, It was quarto format bound in red cloth, and members copied out the text and embellished it with other photographs of Boudník's prints.

In the fall of 1974, Ludvík Vaculík's samizdat imprint Edice Petlice published a second, expanded version of *The Tender Barbarian*. It was in octavo format bound in green cloth, had a much higher print run than the first edition, and 30 copies included an original monotype from Oldřich Hamera of the Barrandovy Jámy, a photograph of Boudník taken by Ladislav Michálek, and three reproductions of Boudník's prints contributed by me. The original texts, particularly "The Tender Barbarian," were touched up and corrected in a few places, but the main difference is that more anecdotes were added: such as the account of "poets going for beer," the encounter between Miloš Forman and Karel Marysko at The Tomcat ("painmaker"), and "Epilogue" tacked onto "Abdication." The contents were expanded to include the sections "Letters to Friends" and "Fragments of Letters from Libeň" — 33 of Boudník's letters previously published in samizdat. This samizdat edition of *The Tender Barbarian*, minus the letters, formed the basis of the first official publication of the book by Odeon in 1990. Before that, however, Edice Expedice, which was founded by Václav Havel, brought out a number of samizdat editions of *The Tender Barbarian* and an untold number of typewritten copies were produced. The exile publishers Index, located in Cologne, Germany, published a Czech edition, slightly altering the title to *The Tender Barbarians,* and Josef Škvorecký's 68 Publishers in Toronto published it as well. Translations published in the 1980s, into French and German for example, were based on these earlier unofficial editions.

Vladislav Merhaut
April 2019, Prague

ACKNOWLEDGMENTS

This translation is based on the first official publication of *The Tender Barbarian* (*Něžný barbar*) by Odeon in 1990 in Prague, edited by Jiřina Zumrová, with the exception, however, of the final paragraph to "Letter to Those Attending a Vernissage." That comes from a typescript dated 1973 in the archives of Susanna Roth (Hrabal's German translator and close friend) and is found in the most recent version (which leaves out "Epilogue, or Abdication") published in volume 3 of the latest iteration of Hrabal's collected works: *Spisy 3 – Novely,* edited by Václav Kadlec and Jiří Pelán, 199-248, Prague: Mladá fronta, 2015.

The texts by Vladimír Boudník come from a variety of sources, and where appropriate were cross-referenced for potential discrepancies in versions. In addition to consulting the original manuscripts and typescripts of the Vladimír Boudník fond in the Museum of Czech Literature Literary Archive, texts were selected from the following publications:

Boudník, Vladimír. *Z Korespondence II (1957-1968).* Edited by Václav Kadlec, Marcela Turečková, and Vladislav Merhaut. Prague: Pražská Imaginace, 1994.

Boudník, Vladimír. *Z Literární pozůstalosti.* Edited by Vladislav Merhaut. Prague: Pražská Imaginace, 1993.

Jednou Nohou, no. 2 (1985).

Larvová, Hana, ed. *Vladimír Boudník 1924–1968.* Prague: Galerie hlavního města Prahy, 1992.

Merhaut, Vladislav. *Grafik Vladimír Boudník*. Prague: Torst, 2010.

Placák, Jan, ed. *Dopisy Vladimíra Boudníka přátelům 1949–1953*. Prague: Ztichlá klika, 2015.

I am deeply indebted to the following for their assistance and support: Tomáš Mazal (Hrabal photos), Vladislav Merhaut, Jan Placák of Ztichlá klika (who provided reproductions for much of the artwork), Misha Sidenberg, the Ministry of Culture of the Czech Republic, and the helpful staff at the Museum of Czech Literature.

J.S.

BOHUMIL HRABAL was born in 1914 in Brno-Židenice, Moravia, and spent his childhood in Nymburk, a place that forms the backdrop for many of his stories. He came to Prague in the late 1930s to study at the Law School of Charles University, settling permanently in the city after the Second World War. An initial flirtation with Surrealism and poetry gave way to "Total Realism" and a focus on prose, which drew on his time working at the Kladno steelworks in the 1950s. Over the subsequent decades he held a variety of jobs while continuing to write a great number of stories and novels. Considered a major stylistic innovator and one of the greatest Czech writers of the 20th century, among his most renowned works are *Closely Watched Trains, I Served the King of England*, and *Too Loud a Solitude*. In February 1997, Hrabal flew out of his hospital window while feeding the pigeons never to return.

VLADIMÍR BOUDNÍK was born on March 17, 1924, in Prague. Sent to Nazi Germany as a forced laborer, after the war he studied at the State School of Graphic Arts and then worked as a graphic designer in a state enterprise's publicity department, a job he eventually quit to work in a factory as a toolmaker. Throughout the 1950s he focused on experimental printmaking, often using factory materials that took the form of active and structural prints, and publicly promulgated his Explosionalist art movement by interacting with factory workers, psychiatric patients, and the general public in the form of street "happenings." His work finally started to receive recognition in the 1960s with a number of exhibitions both at home and abroad. He died of self-strangulation on December 5, 1968.

VLADISLAV MERHAUT met Vladimír Boudník at the ČKD plant in the 1950s and kept a diary on him from 1960 until his death. A founder of the Vladimír Boudník Friendship Society, he has written widely on Boudník's life and works and has edited a few volumes of his correspondence and other texts. His Boudník diary was published in 1997.

JED SLAST is a native of Richmond, Virginia, and longtime Prague resident. His translations from Czech tend to focus on the interwar avant-garde and include *Edition 69, Dreamverse*, and *A Prague Flâneur*.

THE TENDER BARBARIAN
(Pedagogic Texts)
by Bohumil Hrabal

Originally published in Czech as
Něžný barbar (Pedagogické texty), 1974, 1990

Explosionalist texts and artwork by Vladimír Boudník
Afterword by Vladislav Merhaut
All texts translated from the Czech by Jed Slast
Typeset in Garamond Pro / Univers

Flyleaves: Vladimír Boudník on the street, 1955

IMAGE TO WORD 5

TWISTED SPOON PRESS
P.O. Box 21 – Preslova 12
150 00 Prague 5
Czech Republic
www.twistedspoon.com
info@twistedspoon.com

Distributed to the trade by
CENTRAL BOOKS
www.centralbooks.com

Printed and bound in the Czech Republic by Protisk

FIRST EDITION 2019